NATURALLY
GIFTED

A SELF-DISCOVERY
WORKBOOK

Gordon & Rosemary Jones

INTERVARSITY PRESS
DOWNERS GROVE, ILLINOIS 60515

InterVarsity Press® is the book-publishing division of InterVarsity Christian Fellowship®, a student movement active on campus at hundreds of universities, colleges and schools of nursing in the United States of America, and a member movement of the International Fellowship of Evangelical Students. For information about local and regional activities, write Public Relations Dept., InterVarsity Christian Fellowship, 6400 Schroeder Rd., P.O. Box 7895, Madison, WI 53707-7895.

All Scripture quotations, unless otherwise indicated, are taken from the HOLY BIBLE, NEW INTERNATIONAL VERSION®. NIV®. Copyright © 1973, 1978, 1984 by International Bible Society. Used by permission of Zondervan Publishing House. All rights reserved.

The life patterns exercise in chapter four has been adapted from the personal motivation profile developed by Joel Warkentin of Wycliffe Bible Translators.

The interest test in appendix three and the learning type test in appendix seven are copyright Gordon Jones, 1990, and are published by Hatters Lane Publications.

The self/other-esteem measure test in appendix eight is adapted from the self-esteem inventory developed by Dr. Kenneth L. Williams of Wycliffe Bible Translators.

The values card sort test in chapter five and the natural aptitudes card sort in appendix five are based on ideas underlying the work published by Career Research and Testing, 1190 South Bascom Avenue, Suite 214, San Jose, CA 95128.

Cover photograph: Michael Goss
ISBN 0-8308-1662-3

Printed in the United States of America ∞

Library of Congress Cataloging-in-Publication Data

Jones, Gordon, 1937-
    Naturally gifted: a self-discovery workbook/Gordon and Rosemary
Jones.
      p.   cm.
    Includes bibliographical references.
    ISBN 0-8308-1662-3
    1. Self-perception—Religious aspects—Christianity. 2. Self-
report inventories. 3. Ability—Testing. 4. Individuality.
5. Pastoral counseling. I. Jones, Rosemary, 1940- . II. Title.
BV4598.25.J66   1993
248.4—dc20   93-39467
                                        CIP

15	14	13	12	11	10	9	8	7	6	5	4	3	2	1
05	04	03	02	01	00	99	98	97	96	95	94	93		

Preface

This book has arisen out of work with Wycliffe Bible Translators. Their goal is to give the Bible to those who, as yet, do not have the Bible in their own mother tongue. There are nearly six thousand Wycliffe members working in over fifty countries. In trying to help people find work assignments that are fulfilling to them and that increase their effectiveness, a career counseling service has been developed within Wycliffe.

Throughout most of our twenty-five years in Christian service we have worked very closely together, having a joint ministry. The same is true of this book. It is a product of our joint experience and different gifts. When we started writing the book, Rosemary, who works as a career counselor as does Gordon, was studying for a degree in psychology as well as a counseling certificate. As she was busy, Gordon drafted the initial outline of the book. From then on we worked on the book together. For the sake of clarity we have written in the first person.

This book includes some psychometric tests (measures of human behavior) and is based largely on accepted career counseling methods. For those who are interested, these are discussed in appendix one.

Career counseling follows the rules of confidentiality as for other forms of counseling, and for this reason the real-life illustrations given in this book have been modified so that the "clients" are not identifiable. The type of work they are engaged in, the country they worked in, even their gender may have been changed in order to maintain their anonymity. However, the real-life examples are based on actual people with whom we have worked, both in Wycliffe and in the local church.

Our thanks are due to Jenny Chadwick, author of *Without Jeff,* who was a part of the inspiration to go ahead and write this book, and who has used her writing skills to help us in checking the manuscript and suggesting improvements. Thanks also to Joel Warkentin, career guidance coordinator for Wycliffe International, who trained us in career counseling.

Many others have helped in the production of this book: Pam, who gave technical help on learning styles; Nan, Rachael and Sylvia, who typed the draft into the word processor; our long-suffering family, on whom we try out all our ideas; Di, Joyce, Docco, the students at Wycliffe's training courses and many others who have given us feedback.

Last, but not least, we would like to thank all those who have supported us in our Wycliffe ministry over twenty-five years and without whom this book and all our other work in Christian service would not have been possible.

Gordon and Rosemary Jones

1

Discovering Your Individuality

• • •

*T*here is no one the same as you, there never has been and there never will be. God made you different, individual, unique. When he had made you he threw away the mold! He knows your name and he knows your inmost being (Lk 10:20; Ps 139:13). But some of us do not really know ourselves. Knowing ourselves is part of spiritual growth. Each one of us needs to discover just who we are and which particular talents God has given us. Most people function best and get joy and satisfaction when they are using the abilities that God has given them.

This book is about knowing yourself, about discovering your natural gifts and talents. It is concerned with the ways in which you can use these gifts to serve the Lord, and in so doing find true fulfillment.

Finding Your Natural Gifts
I see no reason to believe that our natural gifts and talents are of any less

interest to God, or are any less spiritual than the "spiritual" gifts. All are given by God, represent the work of the Holy Spirit in our lives, and are capable of glorifying his name and furthering his kingdom. The importance of creation around us is emphasized these days, as is our responsibility to use it wisely and well. People are also a part of God's wonderful creation. It is even more important that we use our lives wisely and well, as God intended.

Many people know themselves fairly well and in their passage through life they quickly spot what sort of abilities they have, and find both work and recreational activities that give them deep satisfaction and pleasure. Some find this more difficult than others. Perhaps appropriate opportunities do not naturally exist for them, or they do not recognize just which skills and gifts they have that are needed in the circumstances around them.

This book uses various tests and measures to help us know ourselves better and find out what are our natural gifts. Like slicing through an orange, which looks different cut from one direction than from another, one test looks at our interests, another at what motivates us, a third at what our values are, a fourth at our basic temperament traits and so on. These results, of course, are not exact in the scientific sense, but we all make such judgments whenever we meet people. We talk about people being "outgoing" or "quiet and shy"; we see people as being "quick with figures" or "good with people."

The major objective of this book is to help you understand yourself better and give you some "tools" so that you can continue to grow in self-knowledge. If you are looking for quick answers, you will be disappointed. If it expands your thinking, helps you to have new attitudes about yourself and what you can do and be in life, then it will have succeeded. I trust it will be a *beginning,* not an *answer,* and that it will unlock some of the potential that sits in your "savings account" waiting to be freed.

Gifts in the New Testament

When we look at gifts in the New Testament, we often think of the "spiritual" gifts listed in 1 Corinthians 12:4-11, or the list in Romans 12:6-8. God's gifts to the church (of apostles, prophets, evangelists, pastors and teachers) are listed in Ephesians 4:11, and 1 Corinthians 12:28 has another list of those God has appointed in the church. Some people have tried to determine some order and structure from these lists; I prefer to see them as the result of God's action on, in and through people, enabling the church to reach the world.

First, we have what God has made us through birth—what he intended us to be—that which we get from our genes. Next comes the effect of our environment—home, school, workplace, culture, life experiences. Each of these helps to determine the person we are. Is this process any less a part of God's work than his original creation of us? "For we are God's workmanship," says Ephesians 2:10. He is sovereign—nothing happens to us unless he permits it.

Nehemiah's time as a cupbearer (probably a senior post with administrative responsibilities) in the king's palace prepared him for his later leadership role in bringing God's people back to Jerusalem and organizing them for rebuilding its walls. Moses' dual training, in Pharaoh's palace and keeping his father-in-law's flock in the land of Midian, prepared him for the task of leading Israel in the wilderness.

When we consider the variety of gifts mentioned in the New Testament, one of the most helpful ways of portraying this is of God's grace pouring on us and through us by his Spirit and so reaching to the church and into the world.

God, in his grace, has given you the natural gifts you have. His grace can cause you to grow and to develop these natural traits and tendencies. New gifts that you never dreamed you had will develop and grow out of existing ones. Still others will be added on. These are the "supernaturals": those which come from God but are not naturally found in you.

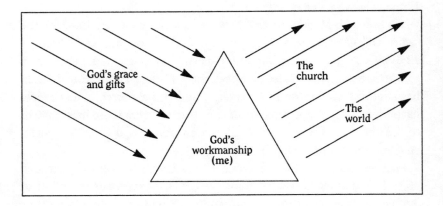

I can find no way of tying God down and making him work in a system. He gives good gifts to his people, for the church. He is sovereign and does so as he wills. Normally, God appears to use our natural traits and gives them a new dimension in his service.

We are God's workmanship. He has made us. We are marred by sin but he seeks to make us like his Son, to be perfected when we go to be with him. We are his instruments. He uses us as we are, with our flaws and failings. He causes us to grow and develop the gifts he has given us for the blessing of the church and for special service. He anoints us with special gifts "so that the body of Christ may be built up" (Eph 4:12).

Spiritual and Natural Gifts

There has been a much greater emphasis on spiritual gifts in our churches in recent years. This book majors on our natural gifts; but does the Bible distinguish between them? What is the link between the two?

The Bible is very clear that we have different gifts, but are some more "spiritual" than others? The interesting thing is that the Bible does not appear to distinguish between spiritual and natural gifts. In our study of spiritual gifts we tend to forget or undervalue some of the gifts that are listed. This is not scriptural, as 1 Corinthians 12 clearly teaches that all the body parts need each other.

Paul does say, however, that we should try to excel in gifts that build up the church (1 Cor 14:12) and eagerly desire spiritual gifts, especially the gift of prophecy (1 Cor 14:1). Two of the lists of gifts in the New Testament contain gifts that we may tend to think of as natural, mixed in with those we think of as spiritual. The Bible appears to see both as spiritual.

In Romans 12:6-8, prophesying, which no one would dispute is a spiritual gift, is followed by serving, teaching, encouraging, contributing to the needs of others, leadership and showing mercy. All of these could be considered natural gifts. Perhaps they become spiritual gifts when dedicated to the Lord and empowered or energized by the Spirit. The gifts mentioned in 1 Corinthians 12:28 are mostly those we would consider as spiritual, but among them are listed "those able to help others" and "those with gifts of administration." These appear to me to be very similar to the more "natural" gifts in Romans 12.

Out of my involvement with the charismatic renewal movement for over twenty years, personal observation tells me that there is often a link between people's personality type—their natural gifts—and the spiritual gifts they exercise. The one usually seems to flow from the other—and the boundary between the two is not always clear-cut!

Some Christians wonder whether we are entitled to find happiness and fulfillment in our lives. Certainly, economic circumstances and other factors often prevent people from being able to utilize fully all the gifts that they have. Happiness is not necessarily a right; we cannot demand of God that we always have meaningful activity.

I'm Not Very Interesting!
You may think that you haven't any specific gifts to offer in God's service, like one lady who came for career counseling. She didn't know herself

very well, and started her initial interview by saying, "You won't find me very interesting." She had a young family and had been a school welfare assistant with some general secretarial experience. As the picture began to unfold, it became obvious that she had quite considerable academic ability. The tests used showed her to have an "academic comfort" (not necessarily IQ, but the degree to which one is at ease in an academic environment) equivalent to that of a university lecturer.

As we looked back on her life and found the things that interested her at school, we found that she loved doing math in school and delighted in puzzling her way through to find the answers. We also discovered that she loved doing jigsaw puzzles in her spare time. The result of our work together was that she went away with new possibilities regarding her future career.

She had never recognized that her investigative, "working out" mind was a gift that could be used in computer programming or in many other scientific and investigative occupations. She was unable to change to a new occupation immediately because of her family commitments, but she was able to prepare for it by reading and by taking short courses. Instead of feeling frustrated and bored, she began to feel a sense of deep satisfaction as she realized that this was the way God had made her and that he intended her to use her gifts.

Does God Use Our Natural Talents?

Great men of the Bible also had a feeling of inadequacy when God chose them for his service in a particular way, and they tended to respond, "Who, *me?* Who am I?" As I have looked more carefully at these stories, it seems to me that their feeling of inadequacy did not mean that they didn't have embryonic natural gifts—they already had the potential for the tasks God had in store for them.

The story of the call of David and his initiation into God's special service is in 1 Samuel 16 and 17. When Samuel asked Jesse, "Are these all the sons you have?" Jesse said, "There is still the youngest, but he is tending the sheep." The youngest can get overlooked in any family; he is always the baby, while the older, more mature siblings have precedence and initially more experience. This does not mean that the youngest is not naturally gifted. We read that David was "ruddy, with a fine appearance." The point is that one wouldn't normally choose the youngest son (he was still a boy) to fight a massive giant of a man, who had been fighting as a warrior since his youth. Even less would anyone have imagined David as king of Israel, but God knew what was in him; God was the Creator of all that David was.

David had proved that the Lord could deliver him from "the paw of the bear," and he believed that God would deliver him from Goliath. He trusted in God. He was offended at Goliath's mocking of God and Israel. While his family and others only saw a young inexperienced boy, God knew David's potential. He chose him as king of Israel and knew he could defeat the Philistine *because* David had a track record of trusting God and allowing him to use him. David had been killing lions and bears for some time with God's help. God trusted David and David trusted God.

We would probably not have chosen David to kill Goliath or to lead Israel. There were lots of stronger and more experienced men around, but David trusted God and wanted to serve and honor him. From God's perspective he was the obvious man for the job. God knew David's potential, which, when yielded back into God's hands, would make him the greatest king Israel ever had. God did not despise what he had made. He did not see only an inexperienced youth.

You may remember Gideon's excuse that he was unfit for God's task: "My clan is the weakest in Manasseh, and I am the least in my family" (Judg 6:15). However, when the angel came to Gideon, he said, "The LORD is with you, mighty warrior" (v. 12). Gideon did not dispute the fact that he was a mighty warrior, but he couldn't believe that God was with Israel and, by implication, with him. "If the LORD is with us, why has all this happened to us?" (v. 13) he asked. This was quite a reasonable reaction for someone whose land was dominated by an enemy power.

God's reply was, "Go in the strength you have and save Israel out of Midian's hand. Am I not sending you?" (v. 14). God was saying, in effect: "You have all the strength you need, Gideon, if I am with you and am sending you." This was the point of difficulty for Gideon. He was not sure of God's desire to save Israel and to use him. This was why he eventually put out a fleece, to convince himself that God was with him and with Israel. When looking at the task of throwing off a strong oppressor, it was natural for him to have self-doubt (v. 15).

Gideon had adequate natural gifts. God knew what was in him. God knew that when Gideon was convinced of his desire to save Israel, he would let him work in him and through him. Then Gideon would be the man for the job. Of course, Gideon felt inadequate for such a huge task.

I have seen many people offered new and challenging assignments in Wycliffe. Almost all question their giftedness for the task, but they do have natural gifts. If God is calling them, and they are willing to be led and strengthened by him, then their natural gifts can be used by him for great things that glorify his name and extend his kingdom.

We need faith to believe that God has faith in us, faith in his creation (which we are). We need faith to believe that the embryonic gifts that he has put in us can grow and yield a rich harvest in his service if we trust him and allow him to use us. Yes, it's scary. It's risky. David and Gideon both went out and risked. They weren't empty people with no gifts. They knew they couldn't do the tasks in their own strength. They needed God with them, releasing their gifts.

Our Preferences
Each of us is born with certain preferences. These preferences and skills help to create a picture of who we are and what our gifts are. Some have a preference for artistic creativity, some for practical activity, some for

logical thinking. If people who do not have much preference for artistic creativity are placed in a situation that requires this ability, then they will soon become uncomfortable as they find themselves unable to function in this area. Similarly, people placed in situations requiring practical skills or logical thinking skills will find it hard if they have no preference for these abilities. If we recognize that we are operating in a situation that is not natural to us, using skills for which we do not have a preference, then we can either move from the situation or learn to live with it. In the latter case we may choose to exercise our natural preferences in other areas of our lives.

There are some simple measures that you can use, which we have included in this book, to help you find your gifts. When you have read and worked through them, you may not have any specific answers at your fingertips, but you should have gained some new insights about your extremely complex personality. Your basic traits are likely to last throughout your life, but God is in the process of molding you into his likeness and, as he is the God of miracles, we should never be surprised when we see changes happening.

Reasons for Seeking Career Help

People these days often have as many as four or five career changes within a lifetime. In years gone by, a man became a carpenter for life, for instance, but not so today. Midlife, for both men and women, sometimes brings a deep desire to develop talents other than those used previously. Many married women have raised a family, which has taken most of their time and emotional energy. Once their children have become independent, they are free to take further training and develop careers. This gives them deep satisfaction for the latter part of their lives.

Other people, for other reasons, may also reach a "midlife crisis" and become aware of a need for a change of direction. Many people who have used their major talent for the first half of their life, be it administration, management or whatever, in the latter half of life seem to want to develop another side of their personality. They often turn to more caring, nurturing aspects of life, whether at home, in voluntary work, or in the caring professions.

Some people turn to the ordained ministry, with the desire to pastor and care for others, or to probation work, teaching or something similar. There is a real joy in discovering the deep hidden talents, motivations and capacities that lie within us all. Far from being a strain, the development of these seems to release floods of new energy.

An increasing number of retired people want to work part time or in a voluntary capacity. They will be seeking help to know what they can do with this part of their lives.

Square Pegs in Round Holes

Unfortunately some Christians find themselves working in totally inappropriate situations, and consequently they suffer unnecessary pain and stress. For instance one woman had been on overseas service, responsible for the literacy programs and development of a wide area. After about two years she was at the end of herself, feeling that she was a failure and that things just were not working out for her. As we worked our way through the career counseling program, several things emerged. Her first and primary gift was that of a "nurturer." From early childhood she cared for individuals and sought to comfort, teach and help them. She was able to recall how she had helped an immigrant child in her own class. This child had been shunned by others, but she was able to befriend her.

Later she earned an M.A. in literacy and eventually specialized in literacy work. She had a great desire to help people and felt she wanted to use her literacy skills to help people overseas. When she arrived at her destination, the hard-pressed, overburdened mission administration thought this "literacy expert" was the solution to all their problems. Immediately, they put her in charge of a whole area where she had to oversee and push forward the literacy work. Her natural learning pattern was to work alongside someone and to learn the ropes, but in this case she was just handed the job on a plate and expected to develop it herself.

The job involved developing liaisons with other missionaries and government bodies, coordinating activities, administering and setting up programs. This woman, who had lovingly cared for and nurtured individuals, or trained and taught small groups, was seeking to use a totally different set of gifts and strengths from the ones with which she had been endowed. Trying to do this over a long period of time had naturally led to disillusionment and stress. I hope this book will help you to avoid being such a square peg in a round hole.

Discovering Your Individuality

I once heard a sermon entitled "Who Am I?" This was given by a minister who obviously had a more introspective personality than I have. My immediate reaction was that it was not a question I would ever bother to ask myself. In fact, he prefaced his sermon with the statement, "Many of us have probably asked ourselves: 'Who am I?' " but the thought had never occurred to me. On reflection I believe that many people *do* ask this question. Some ask it much later in life, while others ask the question from the beginning to the end of their lives.

I believe it is important that each of us finds out just who we are, what God has created us for and what natural gifts he has given us. We may not be able to see all our gifts being used at one time, but self-knowledge does help to explain why we find some tasks tiring, others frustrating and some more difficult than others. We are less likely to criticize ourselves or be self-condemning when we don't function well in certain situations if we realize that we are not using our natural gifts in them.

If we take a piece of machinery or a tool and use it incorrectly or for the wrong purpose, it is damaged and either malfunctions or fails to work at all. Human beings can be damaged similarly. We lack joy and satisfaction and cease to function as whole human beings when the natural talents that God has given us are frustrated and unable to be used, or when we are expected to operate using gifts that are not naturally ours.

As part of my work I am called on to give counsel and guidance to people in full-time Christian service. In some instances they are people who have been unhappy in their work, and as a result have developed a poor self-image and have been at the point of giving up. It has been a great joy to see such people receiving guidance and being helped to understand themselves better. Gradually they see why what they have been doing has been causing stress and frustration. They gain a better understanding of who they are and how they function best. Then they take up new tasks that give them joy, satisfaction and a sense of achievement.

Talking Points

At the end of each chapter there are questions and suggested activities that can be used to stimulate group discussion. Some of the questions and activities will require skill on the part of a group leader, and some will require a high degree of trust between group members. For this reason, choose the questions to suit your particular situation. We would encourage you to use the Bible as the basis for your discussion and to help you find the answers. The group leader will need to research these questions in the Bible first in order to facilitate the discussion.

1. Is there a difference between spiritual and natural gifts, and if so, what?

2. Are Christians entitled to fulfillment in their work or in their lives in general?

3. If you feel you are a "square peg in a round hole" at work, should you "sit it out," believing this is God's place for you, or should you leave because you do not believe the gifts God has given you are being adequately used? What other options are there?

4. Is it important to know what your gifts are? What do you do with this information when you have it? Is discovering your gifts something you do once or is it a lifetime's work?

5. Do you feel that you have been able to be the real "you"? Discuss as a group the degree you feel you have been able to express your real self at home, at school or in the church. In which areas do you feel frustrated, and what plans do you have to change the situation if you feel change is God's way for you?

2

God's
Tasks
for You

• • •

*T*he Bible teaches that we are meant to find satisfaction in work. It is assigned to us by God. Ecclesiastes 5:19 tells us that for a person to "accept his lot and be happy in his work—this is a gift of God," and Ecclesiastes 2:24 states that "a man can . . . find satisfaction in his work. This too, I see, is from the hand of God."

God, when he created us, meant for us to have meaningful activity. Nevertheless, in a fallen world many people are working at jobs that give them little or no satisfaction at all. I have seen people in the Third World picking over a garbage dump to get a few cans, a bottle or two, or gathering paper together to resell. It yields a small amount of money to obtain necessities for themselves and their families. They have little opportunity to find work or the means to buy food in any other way. It's difficult to believe that this is a satisfying job; it certainly wouldn't be to me.

I have no desire to overstate the value of work. Even in our Western society some work is dreary, monotonous and burdensome. However, the main thrust of Ecclesiastes is that *without God* life is meaningless. Nothing gives satisfaction unless we also know him. We need God to enter into our working lives as much as into the other aspects of our lives.

Finance permitting, most people work more for satisfaction than for money. You may find it hard to believe this, particularly on a Monday morning when you face another week and could think of many other things you would rather be doing. I have talked to many people about their work, both in the Christian and in the secular sphere, and to both Christians and non-Christians. My experience is that people get a lot more from their work than just their pay.

Dimensions of Work

The most basic reason for working is to provide us with the things we need in life (food, shelter and so on) and many other things we want, even if we don't need them. As one bumper sticker has it, "I owe, I owe, it's off to work I go." That sums up why many people work—to pay the bills!

Work has also become a measure of our worth in society. The bigger the paycheck and the more prestigious the job, the more valuable we are. Many press their employer for a raise not primarily because they need more money but because they think they are being undervalued.

Work can be a measure of our self-esteem. We often describe people by what they do: "He's a bank manager," or "She's a research scientist." When people retire they sometimes suffer badly from a loss of identity and a feeling of a loss of worth. This is also true of unemployed people. In recent years we have seen people, interviewed on TV, describing the psychological distress they have suffered because of redundancy. It's not the financial loss that seems to cause the greatest stress but the damage to their self-image.

Work gives a sense of achievement. Monsieur Eiffel was probably inordinately pleased with his tower. Many people can look back on certain things they have done and still feel a sense of accomplishment many years later. Even something rather dreary, like clearing out the basement, makes us feel good when it is finished.

The reasons listed so far focus on how work affects us personally, but work is also a means of service. We can work to help others, whether professionally or in our family, church or community. We are often able to give more time to these other aspects of work as we get older and our own financial and achievement needs have been met.

But for many of us work is not a good experience. TGIF (thank goodness it's Friday) sums up a common experience. For others Friday is POETS day (push off early, tomorrow's Saturday). Work is often highly stressful, and we can arrive home exhausted and drained. Alternatively, our work is boring and monotonous and the day is spent waiting for five o'clock when we can leave and do the things we want to do.

Those who work in a voluntary capacity are sometimes made to feel that their work is of less value than if they were paid. This is even more the case for those who stay at home looking after a family. When asked if they work they sometimes say, "No, I'm just a housewife!" Yet if we measured the skills and energy involved in running a home and bringing up a family, they would equate with some very responsible jobs in industry and commerce.

Leisure

The very word *leisure* suggests something of less value and less importance than work. The Christian church has had some negative views on leisure over the centuries. Let us look at what we mean by leisure. If work—defined as what we have to do—is at one end of the spectrum, then at the other end we have what we choose to do, our free time. Of course, there are a host of things that fall between the two. It is difficult to separate leisure and work, and the two form a whole. As in the case of Eiffel, meaningful work is pleasurable.

Leisure has many possible definitions, but the following three give a broad overview. Leisure is, first, our free time, with no obligations. We can do what we like—sit by the TV, go for a walk or just do nothing.

Second, leisure is what we do when we aren't at work, those activities we *choose* to do: hobbies, sports, social activities and even chores. We can choose whether to mow the lawn or fix the front gate.

Third, leisure has to do with the quality of life—that which gives life meaning. It involves our relationships, and in particular our relationship with God. Leisure is relaxation from work, but it is more. Leisure is entertainment, but it is still more. Leisure can be a time for creative expression, a part of God's purpose for us, as in great works of art or music.

Work Is God's Invention

This book is about all that we do in life—both work and leisure. I prefer to use the word *tasks* to describe the things we do. If I use the word *work,* then for some of you it has negative and limited connotations. Some of you may feel that the word *tasks* sounds even more onerous and negative!

I am not sure that God has such a sharp distinction as we sometimes have between work and leisure. Work, sleep, relaxation, family time, relationships, time for others, time in our church, time with God, time to find out who and what we are and what he means us to do with our lives—all are valid uses of time. There are many other tasks we do that are necessary and a part of God's purpose for us. Perhaps we should go back to the beginning of Genesis to see something of God's purpose for us in creating us.

God *worked* at creation for six days (Gen 2:2). God didn't need to work. That would be an inadequate theology. God chose to work and create the world. It gave him pleasure. It was good, and I believe that we can infer that God was pleased. "God saw all that he had made, and it was very good" (Gen 1:31).

Right at the beginning of the creation story we see God giving Adam and Eve tasks; we know that this was good for them, part of what they were created for, and we can be sure it gave them satisfaction and purpose. Men and women are made in God's image. God is Creator and Sustainer of the universe. We are a part of that creation and have a purpose and function in it. The Westminster Catechism states that the function of humankind is "to glorify God and enjoy him for ever." However, glorifying God is not just praising and worshiping him with our lips, or indeed with our minds and bodies. All that we are and all that we do should glorify God.

Humankind's Task

Humans were also given the task of naming all the creatures on the earth. "So the man gave names to all the livestock, the birds of the air and all the beasts of the field" (Gen 2:20). Adam and Eve were not simply to take care of the garden, merely to maintain the status quo, but to continue God's creative work.

"God blessed them and said to them, 'Be fruitful and increase in number; fill the earth and subdue it' " (Gen 1:28). When you think of the size of the earth—its mountains, deserts, jungles—and just two people in it to subdue it, that was quite a big task to give them! Humankind has been doing it ever since, both before the Fall and after it. How much did the Fall modify this task given to man and woman?

The curse contained several elements:

Cursed is the ground because of you; through painful toil you will eat of it all the days of your life. It will produce thorns and thistles for you, and you will eat the plants of the field. By the sweat of your brow you will eat your food until you return to the ground, since from it you were taken; for dust you are and to dust you will return. (Gen 3:17-19)

Adam and Eve were banished from the Garden lest they eat of the tree of life and live forever. There is no reason to believe that the curse took away God's original purpose for them. It obviously modified it, restricted it and placed it in a more controlled environment. The earth was not going to yield their food so easily. Much of their time and energy (the "sweat of your brow" as God said to Adam) was to be given to this.

After the Fall

Originally, perhaps, the Garden and the earth would have yielded food very easily and the man and woman would have had much more time and energy to "subdue the earth" and enjoy the world around them (was this "leisure"?). After the Fall humans needed to use much more time and energy getting food and meeting survival needs. Because God's purpose in giving us work is marred by the Fall, it does not mean it is lost altogether. After the Fall work was no longer just an expression of a person's being. Work became a necessity.

Perhaps today, more than ever, we are seeing that God has called us to the proper use of the earth. The study of ecology has to do with looking after God's world. Our secular work is part of subduing and looking after God's world. Even the rebellious world glorifies God (Ps 68:18). The whole world belongs to God. He is sovereign of both the good and the bad; of those who love him and those who don't; of things that please him and things that don't.

All people, not just Christians, continue to work first for food and other physical necessities, and then to subdue the earth. The advances in medical science are part of humankind's subduing the earth. The advances in other scientific knowledge are also part of it. Some people get great satisfaction studying biology, chemistry, mathematics and a host of other subjects, while others get great fulfillment expressing the caring aspect of God's nature as teachers, nurses and so forth, and still others from acts of creativity of every conceivable sort.

When we make something and it's used properly, it usually gives us satisfaction. God made us as his creation and when we fulfill his purpose for us, this must be pleasing to him. When people work well and get joy using the natural talents God has given them, functioning as he intended, then surely God is pleased. This is his will.

It's unfortunate when we see only "spiritual activities" as of value to God and infer that secular work is somehow materialistic and not pleasing to God. If everyone in the United States ceased their secular work tomorrow, there would be great hardship and even death in our community and in the world.

Full-Time Christian Service

There is a great need for people to engage in Christian work, both full time and in our spare time, both in the local church and in the church overseas, but it's wrong to infer that a daily secular task is any less pleasing to God. It is wrong to damage or destroy the joy in that service by suggesting that it is not God's design, purpose or pleasure. This comes from a limited view of God's tasks for us.

If we belong to the Lord, then everything we do is Christian service, be it "secular" or "religious." Christians are called to total commitment to God. "I have been crucified with Christ and I no longer live, but Christ lives in me" (Gal 2:20). Jesus walked about Galilee and Judea being full-time for God. Earning a living is full-time service for God when our lives are committed to him. Without committed Christians in secular employment the established "religious" institutions—churches, missionary societies and other parachurch groups—would not be able to function. They would have no money!

Jesus served God in the carpenter's shop just as much as he served him during his three-year peripatetic ministry prior to his death. Nevertheless we need terminology to describe Christian employment and those Christians who work in secular employment. The danger is in suggesting that one is more godly, or of more value. The term "full-time" is unfortunate since it suggests that others serve God part time. If I use the term "paid Christian employment" then some will say they are not paid but live by faith. When we use the term "live by faith" we obviously don't want to suggest that others *don't* live by faith. I prefer to use the more traditional terms simply for ease of communication, providing it is clear that by so doing I am not denigrating the service of others.

We need Christians in full-time work. The task is huge both at home and overseas. We need Christians sent out and equipped to serve God overseas, taking his Word and the message of reconciliation to a needy world. We also need Christians in ordinary secular jobs, demonstrating God's love in them. They are there as his witnesses, but not just as his witnesses. They are part of God's world, part of his creation, subduing the earth.

Honoring God in Ordinary Tasks

This is not the place to argue about whether people should only "stay at home" if they are unable to "serve overseas." Many can't serve overseas, or even in full-time service in the United States. They are debarred by temperament, physical strength or well-being, education, skills, or whatever and therefore serve in secular work at home.

When we share with Christians about the need for full-time workers, we should be careful that we don't cause those not called to this to feel second rate, that their jobs are not so important to God. We should never imply that we are at work only to witness and to tell others of him in the workplace, or only to earn money to keep house and family or to support missions. All our jobs have value in their own right. If God has called you to a "secular" task, then that is God's calling for you. Do it well and enjoy it. As 1 Corinthians 10:31 says, "Whether you eat or drink or whatever you do, do it all for the glory of God."

Successful Organizations

The key to every successful organization is people functioning well. If a local company, manufacturing and selling double-glazing, for example, is successful, then you will probably find that people within it are using their natural gifts well. When people are working well, the organization will function effectively and achieve its purpose and goals.

What of the Holy Spirit? you may ask. Surely when the Holy Spirit works through people then God's work is done? True, but he usually works in and through our natural gifts as well as in a more direct way.

Successful Churches

Ralph Mattson and Arthur Miller, two Christian men engaged in career counseling work in the United States, state in their book *Finding a Job You Can Love* that "the church that is successful does well because God-given gifts have been placed suitably and are functioning properly."[1] Obviously, this is not the only reason—or we could simply call in some management experts and career guidance counselors to see that everyone in the church functions in the role that most closely matches their gifts and talents, and the church would be successful. There are more ingredients than this to a successful church, a successful mission or indeed any venture for God. Nevertheless it must be pleasing to God to see his people harness and use the gifts and talents he has given them for his service, harmonizing one with another as parts of a body, each one complementing the others so that as a whole they have all the gifts that are needed.

A study by the Marketing and Research Corporation showed that three or four out of every five people were in the wrong jobs.[2] Statistics are always difficult to interpret, but whatever interpretation we put on this it's probably true that many people do not maximize their potential in life in general and in their work in particular.

What of the church? What sort of a labor force do we have? Fifty, one hundred, two hundred people perhaps giving five, ten or even fifteen hours per week each? What a management exercise! Helping each one find the best slot in the body so that what they do gives them joy and satisfaction, not only because it's for the Lord, not only because it furthers his kingdom, but because they feel that they are using the gifts and talents that he has given them—that's some task!

Judgment and Rewards

The parables of the talents (Mt 25) and of the minas (Lk 19) show us that what the Lord has given us, he expects us to use, not hide away and bury. Those who used their talents or minas well were rewarded. He who hid his talent or mina and didn't use it was rebuked. In both parables those who used their resources well were given further responsibility.

We must recognize that the Bible speaks of a judgment of Christians and of what they have done with their lives. We are accountable to God for what he has given us in gifts and talents; we shall be asked what we have done with them.

When Christ returns and we stand before him, what will he say to you: "Well done, good and faithful servant! You have been faithful . . . I will put you in charge of many things. Come and share your master's happiness!" (Mt 25:23) or "You wicked, lazy servant" (v. 26)? It's clear that God expects us to make good use of what he has given us, not because we fear judgment at the end of time but because in so doing we show that we want to serve him because we love him.

God's desire is to encourage us rather than to judge us. We all need affirmation and encouragement in our work. We should not be surprised when the secular business world discovers this truth and begins putting it to work. The question was asked of the chief executive of a leading multinational company: "What is the most important talent you look for in a manager/executive?" The answer: "The ability to affirm and encourage subordinates." Does that surprise you? God the Father affirmed Jesus when he said, "This is my Son, whom I love; with him I am well pleased" (Mt 3:17).

The Well-Motivated Christian

Mattson and Miller paint a good picture of well-motivated Christians maximizing their potential for God.

He is the person whose work fits his gifts and who demonstrates the harmony between man and work that God intends for his people. He enjoys his work and can be affirmed in it, and thereby becomes attractive to the people around him.

He knows his gift comes from the Lord and is not of his own making, so he visibly shows the grace of God in his life and gives praise to God. He knows that even if he is working for a secular business, the principles by which that business has any cohesion at all are God's creation; and he knows that all the distortion of God's purpose expressed by that particular business cannot dim the reality that no God means no business. . . .

Integrating his faith in his work can bring an infusion of new vitality to both faith and work. Knowing that work lies at the center of his calling will enliven his faith and revive a sense of gratitude, which will in turn draw him closer to the Lord.[3]

In a fallen world the above is not going to be true of all of us. Some will, through no fault of their own, be unable to "succeed" in the world of work; but, like the man with one talent, we are still to seek to use it and not give up and bury it. We will not love God with all our heart nor love our neighbors as ourselves; we shall not make perfect marriages and we won't be perfect parents, *but* we are to try to do so.

We shall not always use our gifts well—our careers will go awry. We will not always fit well into the local church or find our niche in Christian service. But we should recognize that God's purpose is for us to seek to do so with his help. When we fail to fit in effectively, we need to ask God's forgiveness and consciously seek his grace and help to try again.

This book is for you to read, think about and discuss with your friends. However, it is more than that. It is a workbook with exercises for you to do. As you do these, a profile of yourself should emerge. It would be a good idea to get a folder in which to keep your results. Label each set of results clearly so that you can refer to them when you are ready to complete your profile.

Talking Points

1. Does the Bible draw a distinction between spiritual and secular work?

2. Is leisure as much a part of God's design for us as is work? Is he interested in your enjoyment of life or only in the things you can do for him?

3. Is the concept of full-time Christian service valid? Can you think of a better term to describe those who enter Christian service as a full-time occupation?

4. Do you need a "call" to Christian service, or is the need a call in itself? Do you need a "call" to "stay at home" or to do a secular job?

5. What does it mean in Genesis 1:28 when God said to Adam and Eve that they should "subdue the earth"? Have we been too enthusiastic in our "subduing the earth," and does it include taking good care of the earth? Whose responsibility is the earth?

6. What was the effect of the Fall on God's purpose for humankind? How are the tasks God intended for us affected? Does it mean work is no longer enjoyable?

7. Does God have a particular plan for our lives, or does the "freedom of choice" that God has given us include freedom to choose how we should spend them? How should we set about choosing what we should do with our lives?

3
Interests

● ● ●

*M*ost of us sparkle when we get onto our favorite topic or hobbyhorse, because the subject really interests us. Similarly it has been found that each of us has certain work or occupational interests for which we have an affinity. This is nothing new; very early in the Bible individuals had specialized roles. For example, we read in Genesis 4:19-22 that Jabal "was the father of those who live in tents and raise livestock. His brother's name was Jubal; he was the father of all who play the harp and flute. Zillah also had a son, Tubal-Cain, who forged all kinds of tools out of bronze and iron." It would be wrong to infer too much from verses such as these, but it would seem clear that we can be born with a disposition to certain activities. Even Cain and Abel had different interests, the one in working the soil and the other in keeping the flocks.

In the 1950s R. B. Forer suggested that vocational interests are essentially expressions of personality, an idea that stimulated John Holland to develop the "Vocational Preference Inventory," a simple yet effective personality test consisting entirely of occupational items.

We now come to the first of the tests. To avoid influencing your answers, complete the interest test (appendix three) before reading the different interest types set out below. We have cultural and Christian biases toward certain interests and away from others, and it's important that you answer the questions honestly. In this test, as with the others in this book, it is best to give your immediate "gut-level" answer rather than pore over the questions and try to analyze them too deeply.

Validating Your Test Result

Do you feel the test reflects your interest preferences adequately? It is important that you validate any test results. This means that you agree with them and feel that they adequately represent you. Some of you may get more accurate results by scoring yourself directly against the descriptions below than by doing the test. Tests are most helpful to those who find it difficult to get hold of concepts.

To validate your result, read through the theme descriptions and award yourself points out of ten against each theme, according to the degree to which the theme matches your interest preferences. Please note that pure types do not exist and that these descriptions list *likely* behavior, attributes, occupations and so forth.

Occupational Themes

Realistic—R Theme. These people need to see tangible results from their work. They have a preference for working outside and with tools, machines or animals. They prefer to work with things rather than with people or ideas. They may be described as honest, straight-talking, practical, modest, frugal and conforming. They may find difficulty in expressing their feelings and with verbal communication. They are often found in military or emergency services, agricultural and mechanical work, skilled trade and building environments. Typical Realistic occupations are followed by farmers, mechanics, carpenters, police officers, foresters and general maintenance people.

Investigative—I Theme. These people thirst after knowledge. They want to understand the world about them and study theoretical systems such as biology, physics, mathematics and such. They may be described as precise, independent, intellectually curious, analytical, quiet and reserved, and logical. They enjoy solving abstract problems and facing ambiguous challenges, preferring thinking to doing. They are often seen as "free thinkers" and are uncomfortable with rules and regulations. They are often found in mathematical, scientific, research, medical technology and problem-solving environments. People in typical Investigative occupations are computer programmers, math teachers, biologists and pharmacists.

Artistic—A Theme. These people like to express their individuality. This leads to creativity in the arts (drama, painting, music, writing) and/or in concepts and ideas (architecture). They may be described as idealistic, expressive, dissenting, impetuous, temperamental, complex and creative. They have little interest in the business and commercial world and are often unconventional in dress and lifestyle. They are often found in performing/entertaining, arts/crafts and highly original environments. People in typical Artistic occupations are commercial artists, musicians, photographers, actors and journalists.

Social—S Theme. These people need to help other people. They often have naturally empathetic skills demonstrated in listening to and understanding other people. They seek to nurture, heal and promote growth and wholeness in others. They may be described as sociable, considerate, patient, caring, sympathetic, generous, responsible and cheerful. They prefer to solve problems by discussion with others and are able to handle their own relationships and those between others. They are usually uncomfortable with machines. They are often found in educational, welfare, humanitarian and medical service environments. People in typical Social occupations are social workers, nurses, primary teachers, counselors and pastors.

Enterprising—E Theme. These people need to persuade other people to their point of view. This means that they are usually effective in selling, leadership and public speaking. They may be described as industrious, dominant, self-confident, ambitious, influential, in-the-limelight, well-liked and optimistic. They can be impatient with theoretical or detailed work. They like the trappings of authority (status, power, wealth). They are often found in promotional, political, merchandising and business management environments. People in typical Enterprising occupations are real estate agents, retail sales managers, marketing directors, union negotiators and management consultants.

Conventional—C Theme. These people need structure and order. Where these exist they keep to procedures and organizational rules. Where these don't exist they will bring order and system to their environment. They may be described as stable, cautious, systematic, dogged, fastidious, reliable and accurate. They are less interested in individuality than in corporate responsibility. They dislike ambiguity, preferring to know exactly what is required of them. They are often found in office, financial and procedural environments. People in typical Conventional occupations are secretaries, bookkeepers, VDT operators and accountants.

Get a friend or a relative to read through the above occupation themes and give you their estimate of your interest preferences. Place it alongside your self-estimate.

Self/Other Validation Chart

Theme	R	I	A	S	E	C
Self-estimate						
Friend's estimate of me						
Relative's estimate of me						
Total						

Enter these results in the self/other observation boxes on the answer sheet in appendix three.

Different Code Patterns

You may show a clear preference on interest themes. Perhaps you are RC (Realistic-Conventional), a practical person who likes working in a systematic way, following set procedures. The Social, Investigative, Artistic and Enterprising themes may not be very apparent in you.

My own experience is that some people appear to have three groupings: dominant, auxiliary and weak. Dominant themes are probably indicated as those which scored highest in the tests in appendix three; weak themes are those which scored lowest. The dominant are the themes that are our natural interests. We back these up by using the auxiliary themes. Let us take an example:

Dominant	Auxiliary	Weak
RC	SA	EI

You may have RC as your main interest theme. Perhaps you are a carpenter, a window cleaner, a cook or a homemaker, as many domestic crafts have this coding. You may often use your skills to serve or help others, thereby using your Social auxiliary. You may have reasonable creativity in solving practical problems in an imaginative way, thereby using your Artistic auxiliary. You may work in environments or take part in activities best described by the following themes:

RCS, RCA, RSC, RAC, CRS, CRA, CSR, CAR

It is important to take note of our weakest themes as well as of our strongest, that is, what we are not as well as what we are. I recently did career counseling with someone who was using his dominant themes in his job (in this case CR) but was unhappy and finding the job very stressful. In fact, the job had a need for the E theme, managing and directing other staff, and this he found very difficult. It's important, therefore, not only to check that our preferences are used but that our weak areas are not essential to the job.

Exercise with Caution

By means of this composite test you may have been able to determine just where your interest preferences lie. Different tests, which use a different grid to approach these interest themes, might yield slightly different results, because every test has a certain bias. For example, some ask questions about what we can do. You may have been brought up with a practical father who was patient and taught you to fit an electric plug, use a saw, hammer and so forth. Similarly if you had a practical mother you may be good at baking, sewing and such. In either case you may score higher on practical interests than you would if your parents were not practical.

Do remember that this is not an exact science. God hasn't stamped your interest code somewhere on you! You will be as much helped by puzzling through just where your interests lie, and thinking of your family, friends, colleagues and where their interests lie, as by the results of any test.

I am concerned when I hear someone say, "I am an REI," as though these letters run through their bones like letters through seaside rock. We tend to do this when discussing interest themes for ease of communication. A more accurate description would be, "My preference seems to be for Realistic (R) interests. Enterprising (E) seems next, and then Investigative (I)." Of course we all use all six. We couldn't survive in life if we had none of any one of them. We may find our preferences alter with our age or as we go through different phases of life, although research has shown interest themes to be remarkably consistent throughout our lives.

We must remember that no job, and no person, can be exactly categorized by such a coding. It is only a guide to help our thinking. Many people operate quite successfully where their own interest themes do not exactly match the themes of the jobs they are doing. This, in one sense, is good—in that in an office team or research team, each member brings a different approach or a different strength.

Job Categorization

John Holland's work on occupational codes has been widely researched and extensively used. The U.S. Department of Labor uses Holland Codes in its job categorization. The Canadian government has made similar use of Holland's codes. Now check your final agreed code with the occupational listing in appendix four. Obviously, only a few job codes can be listed here, but you should get some idea of the type of areas where your code indicates that you could function naturally. *The Dictionary of Holland Occupational Codes* gives a more complete listing.[1] Do not expect to like or be interested in every job that matches or is near your code; that would be unrealistic. Use the occupational list as a guide to give you some ideas. These should be confirmed, or perhaps rejected, when the data acquired in other chapters are taken into account.

Don't think that your interest themes are the only factor to consider when looking at how you use your life. Your values and your natural aptitudes, which we will cover in further chapters, are also important. My goal is not just that you examine your job but also your tasks (your hobbies, church work and so on) and ensure that you know who you are and, as far as possible, that you are using the talents that God has given you.

Holland's Hexagonal Model

We have sought to measure your interests and the themes that best describe them. Holland postulated interest environments and that people are most at ease working in an environment that matches or approximates their interest type. Since these environments will attract people of similar interests, if we work in these environments we shall be working with those whose interests correspond to our own.

The relationship between the six interest environments differs. This can be neatly represented by writing the letters around a hexagon. If we work around the edge of the hexagon, R and I have a close relationship as do IA, AS, SE, EC and CR.

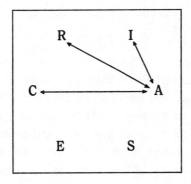

There is a lower level of relationship between RA, IS, AE, SC, ER and CI. There is an even lower level of relationship between RS, IE and AC. This means that an individual's codes are often grouped around the edge of the hexagon, for example, RIA, IAS, ASE, SEC, ECR and CRI.

Where there are only two major interest themes they are likely to be adjacent, such as RI, IA, AS, SE, EC and CR.

Environments (jobs) tend to follow a similar pattern. So we are more likely to find RI jobs, for example, than RS. The former would be represented by many branches of engineering, which have a Realistic as well as an Investigative aspect.

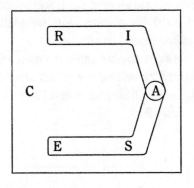

Jobs whose coding is not adjacent seem to occur less often. However, I have met and worked with Realistic (R) people who have a major interest in Social (S) activities. One man I knew was good at fixing things, particularly cars, and loved helping people. He would regularly stop to help a driver stranded by the roadside and got great satisfaction in doing so. I saw an advertisement recently for a job with the automobile association where the applicants needed at least three years of garage experience plus "people skills and a desire to help people." This shows that jobs do exist that cut across the more usual interest patterns—but we should recognize that these jobs are the exception rather than the rule.

Biblical Types

It may seem a bit imaginative to seek to identify interest types among biblical characters. However, we can look at the behavior of people in the Scriptures and see some of the behavior characteristics of the interest types.

Realistic. Practical, often physically stronger than average, good with their hands.

Bezalel and his helper Oholiab were anointed and chosen by God to

---

lead the team of craftsmen to construct the tabernacle and its furniture. "I have filled him [Bezalel] with the Spirit of God, with skill, ability and knowledge in all kinds of crafts—to make artistic designs for work in gold, silver and bronze, to cut and set stones, to work in wood, and to engage in all kinds of craftsmanship" (Ex 31:3-5). "I have appointed Oholiab. . . . Also I have given skill to all the craftsmen" (v. 6).

Realistic people were particularly valued in cultures before the industrial age, because craftsmen like Bezalel and Oholiab were the means of making and producing things. The physically strong, like Samson, led armies and defeated their enemies.

Of course they would also have other interest themes; Bezalel and Oholiab had Artistic type skills as well.

Investigative. Analytical thinker, critical, intellectual.

Paul immediately springs to mind. Apart from his analytical and logical thinking, he also had practical skills—he was a tentmaker. Were his codes RI, those adjacent in the interest hexagon?

Artistic. Emotional, idealistic, impulsive, independent, poetic and musically able.

David, the author of the psalms, the musician whose skill so affected Saul, would appear to have at least some of the Artistic theme characteristics (see 1 Sam 16:23).

Social. Helpful, generous, sociable.

Barnabas, the encourager, got his name because he encouraged so many. It is difficult to imagine anyone getting such a title if he was not naturally gifted at getting alongside people and entering into their lives in a helpful way.

Enterprising. Adventurous, energetic, optimistic, resourceful.

Nehemiah, with his vision and practical abilities to organize and lead, to manage people and projects, must have had some natural enterprising skills to have undertaken the overseeing of the return from exile of the first party of Jews to Jerusalem to rebuild the walls. Remember that

Nehemiah was already cupbearer to the king, a high government administrative office, when we are first introduced to him in the book of Nehemiah.

Conventional. Reliable, accurate, consistent, keen on procedures.

Ezra the scribe has these characteristics listed in my reference Bible: trustworthy, prayerful, self-denying, faithful and honoring God's Word. He sought to lead the Jews of his time back to the true Jewish faith, to worship God according to the fashion laid down by God.

Conventional people are reliable and painstaking, will work long hours with great loyalty to the group or system. They keep the system going and defend the status quo. It's a pity that this theme has so uninspiring a title, particularly so since the church needs its conventionals along with the other five types.

You might like to look at other biblical characters and see if you can identify which interest themes were their preference. It is good to see that God appears to use all six types and combinations of types.

At the end of the book we will be gathering together all your data to form your personal profile. You will need the results of your interest test for this, so put them in your results folder.

Talking Points

1. Which interest theme characteristics are most highly valued in your church, in your school, in your place of work, in our society? How does God value them?

2. Can you think of ways to encourage those with each of the interest themes to use their gifts in your church? For example, where can those with Realistic gifts help? What would be the best use of those with Enterprising gifts?

3. Can you identify a Bible character for each of the six interest themes and say how God used the natural gifts he had given them?

4

Natural
Aptitudes

• • •

*Y*ou may have heard it said, "Oh, he's a natural . . ." about
someone learning to do something: perhaps learning to ride a
horse, drive a car or care for children. We say, "He took to it
like a duck to water." You are good at certain things too, and always have
been. God has given all of us certain gifts, but sometimes the problem
is to discover what these gifts are.

You may have been born with a natural aptitude to organize. If your
main interest is Realistic and you train as a motor mechanic, you could
end up arranging the work schedules in the repair department. If your
main interests are in the Artistic area, and you have the natural aptitude
to communicate, then you may find great satisfaction in doing the art
work for your church's publications.

What Is a Natural Aptitude?
A natural aptitude is popularly understood as an innate ability to perform

in one area or another. In the context of career counseling, natural aptitudes are better known as motivational skills, because having a particular skill motivates us to act in a certain way. They show up early in life and can be used in many different spheres, depending on your values and interests.

Natural aptitudes are sometimes called transferable skills to differentiate them from learned skills. For example, a child who is able to persuade his parents to extend his bedtime may be the best at selling candy for his primary school. In secondary school he may become president of the debate club, and then go on to study sales and marketing at college. Eventually he may become the sales director of some company. His ability to persuade and convince people has always been there but he has used it in different ways.

Similarly, the little girl who plays mother to her dolls and looks after other children in the playground grows up to care for her school friends and their welfare. She trains as a nurse and makes a natural mother when she marries. Later on she develops a counseling ministry in the local church. It is obvious that she was born with and is motivated by a nurturing aptitude or motivating skill. Unfortunately life is not usually so clear-cut, either for ourselves or others, and we may not readily recognize our aptitudes, despite the fact that they are part of our basic personality and motivate us, in that we enjoy doing them, often showing considerable natural skill at them.

Life Patterns Exercise

One possible method of determining your natural aptitudes is by reviewing your past achievements, those which were both enjoyable and satisfying to you. They are likely to be things that you did naturally and easily, or things that maybe caused you to get excited or animated. In retrospect these events still give you a sense of accomplishment and achievement, not because other people approved of them but because you approved of what you did. These should not be enormous undertakings involving many skills, but small things.

Here are some examples of achievements others have used to identify their natural aptitudes.

- ☐ making cakes with Mom for my birthday party
- ☐ choosing the color scheme for my room
- ☐ assisting at the birth of my first child
- ☐ taking over the leadership of the church Sunday school
- ☐ planning a two-week cycling holiday in Scotland
- ☐ gaining compensation for the damage to my suitcase by the airline and negotiating a settlement
- ☐ picking up two elderly ladies and taking them to church each week
- ☐ organizing the Christmas carol service at the school where I work
- ☐ teaching myself to use a computer

How to Record Your Achievements

Try to arrange your achievements under age groupings as follows:

> 5—11 years
> 12—18 years
> 19—25 years
> 26—35 years
> 36—50 years
> 51+ years

If you are in your teens or twenties, split up the age ranges into a smaller number of years. It is good to get two or three activities for each age range. You may find it hard to think back to your early years, but it will probably come back if you are patient. It is helpful and fun to do this with a friend who knows you well and who can trigger your memory about past events.

Parents can be very helpful in remembering your early achievements, but there is one snag. They may recall things that *they* enjoyed you doing and not the things that *you* enjoyed doing. They may have thoroughly enjoyed seeing you as the angel Gabriel in the school nativity play and think that you derived just as much pleasure from playing the part as they did from watching you. Looking back, you recoil in horror at the agonies you went through at the time. You remember how you hated being the center of attention when you sang a solo, and the feeling of utter relief you experienced when the curtain came down on the final act. There was no sense of exhilaration or achievement, so this memory should not be included.

There are some things that we never forget: the thrill of swimming the first unaided strokes across the pool, the delight at passing our driving test first time, or the flush of success at passing a particularly difficult exam. You should avoid including these achievements in your list because while some people are constantly motivated by these personal growth activities, everyone gets some satisfaction from them, so it can bias the result of the inquiry.

When you have listed as many things as you can, take the ten most memorable achievements and put them in order of preference, with the most satisfying first and the least satisfying last. Then take the first six of these and write a fuller description (of about two hundred words) for each achievement. Try to have at least one from the 5—11 years period and at least one from the 12—18 years period.

How to Write Up Your Achievements

The following example shows you how *not* to do it:

> Being made chief mechanic for school go-cart race. I was asked to be chief mechanic for the school twenty-four-hour go-cart race. I enjoyed being part of a team and was pleased when our team won.

The following description is much better as it is more detailed and describes *how* you did things and *what* you did.

> Every year we had a twenty-four-hour interhouse go-cart race. One year

I was asked to be the chief mechanic for our house team. We had to fix up a go-cart so that it could be raced constantly without breaking down. I called a meeting of the team to discuss just what needed to be done to the go-cart. I enjoyed coming up with ideas to strengthen the frame, replace worn cogs, and other repairs. They agreed with many of my recommendations and approved a repair program. I oversaw the welding, arranged to purchase the necessary parts, and set in motion a program to bring the go-cart up to the necessary standard. I painted it in a combination of the school and house colors. On the day of the race I ensured that we had all the necessary tools, oil, etc. I organized a schedule for the team to take turns driving, keeping the best drivers until last. I was pleased when we won because we had worked well as a team and made the best use of our resources. I felt my leadership had been a decisive part in this.

This description is better because it incorporates the way in which the job was tackled and ends by stating how the person felt when he had completed his task. Try to end each description with a statement of how you felt personally satisfied or fulfilled. "I just enjoyed doing it." "They all had a good time." "I felt I had done it myself." "I could see she was feeling better." "I knew I had produced my best."

Are you beginning to discover the natural patterns by which you operate? Isn't our God good to give us these aptitudes that we enjoy using? Your job may be a clerk/typist and if your natural skills are in keeping files and records, counting and classifying, you probably enjoy it. But you will not be very fulfilled if your skills are organizing, making arrangements, investigating or doing research. These are the skills used more by an executive secretary.

Examining Your Achievements
This chapter and the life patterns exercise are the most demanding in the book. At this point you may choose to omit this section on analyzing your

achievements and return to it later. You could continue reading from the section entitled "Natural Aptitudes and Our Christian Commitment." If you do that, be sure to return to this section, as this examination of your achievements is a crucial part of discovering your life patterns, your individual style and your natural aptitudes.

You now need to go back over the six activities you described previously and underline all the verbs that describe what you did and how you did it. These may be implicit rather than explicit, depending on how you wrote them up.

You may wish to add other words to those which you originally underlined in order to give a fuller description of how you did it or what you did. You may wish to use other verbs to help describe the natural aptitude you were using at that time. You should try to get a minimum of twenty verbs describing these natural activities that gave you satisfaction. For example, if you wrote, "I read all the books," read/search/find out are appropriate verbs. If you can find a general term that more adequately describes the natural ability you were using, you could express it, for example, thus: "I wrote . . . I had to telephone as well and later met the person and discussed face to face"; therefore "communicate" (phone, write, discuss) is an appropriate description. Now, underneath each description of an activity, list what natural aptitudes you were using. We are looking at what you did and how you did it, not why you did it. We are looking for the verbs that describe the activity, such as "I organized," "I gathered the data," "I researched the whole subject."

This is a long exercise but it is well worth the effort. Remember, this is your life that you are examining, and that provides the best possible data for determining your natural aptitudes.

Your Natural Way of Doing Things
Try to list these verbs under the three groupings below.

1. What is your natural way of managing your own life? For example,

try/risk/go for it, be confident/positive, take action/do/self-start, be responsible for.

2. How do you interact with people? For example, interact/discuss/exchange ideas, lead/direct/tell, teach/evangelize, build trust/establish friendships.

3. How do you handle the world about you (data, ideas, things)? For example, build/construct, write/telephone, organize/schedule.

Now go back to your six descriptions again and in each one try to determine which environments these activities took place in, such as school/college, home, church, and what sort of environment or activity it was, such as group activity, challenging, intellectually stimulating.

4. In what sort of environment do you normally operate most happily? For example, one where there is variety/flexibility, challenge, new ideas/efficiency/improvement, scope for the artistic/creative, in small groups.

Now examine the six activities again and try to find what objects (or data, concepts and so forth) you worked on.

5. On what sort of objects do you normally work? For example, wood/building materials, people (as in counseling), computers, systems.

To complete your examination of the activities you have done naturally and from which you have gained real satisfaction, you can look at two more areas. First, examine each activity to see if you can determine if you have a natural role or style. Some examples are listed below.

6. What role and/or style do you use? (Your role is what your function is and your style is how you go about doing it.) For example, as a builder/developer, expert, organizer/doer, manager/coach, hands-on activist.

Last, look at what it was that gave you such a sense of satisfaction for each of the six accomplishments. Even though the activities are different, you may find that the "payoff," that is, what made it a satisfying achievement for you, is similar in several of them. We will be looking at these again when we consider values in the next chapter.

7. What motivates you to achieve? (Why you do things—the payoff.) For example, having good fellowship/relationships, experimenting/ investigating by trial and error, being able to do it/exercising competence.

Discerning Your Pattern

I know this is very hard for some of you and that you won't get answers to all the sections. However, the whole exercise of finding your natural patterns should help you. Just examining your preferred spheres of working is enlightening quite apart from any precise final results. You may find it helpful to set out the data you gathered from the six activities as in the table below, to help you gain an overall picture of your natural aptitudes and how and where they operate. List the word or phrase that best sums up your answers to questions four to seven above, and look at each of the top six activities that represent your achievements. The table shows an example of some possible conclusions.

Situation	Environment	Dealing with	Role/Style	Motivation
1	school	wood	creator	to do a good job
2	park	people	organizer	to help them
3	home	people	harmonizer	to help them
4	school	people	teacher	to help them learn
5	office	people	manager	to achieve through people
6	school	people	counselor	to help them grow

Can you see any discernible patterns? Do you have a preferred environment in which to work? Do you naturally like certain things or people with which to deal? Do you have a particular motivating pattern?

Natural Aptitudes and Our Christian Commitment

Why do we want to know our natural aptitudes? So that we may use them and thereby discover some of God's purpose in creating us? Because we shall be more fulfilled and feel more authentic? Yes, but more than these, for Christians live to glorify God, and the more potential they discover in themselves, the more they have to yield for God's use. These natural aptitudes are nearer to the essence of our being than any of the other aspects of personality that we shall consider.

We read of Daniel and his friends as "young men without any physical defect, handsome, showing aptitude for every kind of learning, well informed, quick to understand, and qualified to serve in the king's palace" (Dan 1:4). We know that Daniel was committed to following the Lord—"Daniel resolved not to defile himself" (v. 8). This commitment led God to take these natural aptitudes he had created in Daniel and further use and enhance them for his service.

After keeping God's law and not defiling themselves by eating royal food and wine, we read, "To these four young men God gave knowledge and understanding of all kinds of literature and learning. And Daniel could understand visions and dreams of all kinds" (v. 17). Was God taking their natural "aptitude for every kind of learning" and causing it to grow and develop as they submitted themselves to him? When they entered the king's service we read that "in every matter of wisdom and understanding about which the king questioned them, he found them ten times better than all the magicians and enchanters in his whole kingdom" (v. 20).

We know that Daniel had opportunity to interpret Nebuchadnezzar's dream even when the king wouldn't say what the dream was. This resulted in Daniel being promoted to a position of great responsibility in the kingdom. There were further opportunities for Daniel to exercise these gifts. Of all the great people of the Bible, Daniel stands alone as a man who was totally committed to God. We don't see any major failings, as we do with so many of the other great Bible characters. The word that springs to mind to describe Daniel is "integrity." Daniel's integrity allowed God to take his natural aptitudes and develop them. God caused other people to recognize Daniel's gifts. Later in his life, God also gave Daniel spiritual gifts, obviously above and beyond the natural abilities that men and women can normally exercise.

If we were to begin building a natural aptitudes list from the limited data we have about Daniel, it might read like this:

1. Managing his own life
   read/study/learn, reflect/think
2. Interacting with people
   be open/honest
3. Handling the world around him
   envisage, investigate/find out, administer
4. Natural environments
   literary, intellectual, responsible
5. Natural objects
   books, languages
6. Role/style
   visionary
7. Motivation
   discerning the truth

Of course we don't have enough evidence to complete this accurately, but can you see how God took Daniel's natural aptitudes and caused them to develop to a high degree of skill? God didn't use his physical strength because that was not his natural gift. In Samson's case God used his physical strength and gave him a high degree of natural skill. Used later in the destruction of the Philistine temple, it became a supernatural strength.

David recognized Solomon's natural aptitude for wisdom. In his charge to Solomon he said, "Deal . . . according to your wisdom" (1 Kings 2:6). Also, "You are a man of wisdom; you will know what to do" (v. 9). Solomon committed this wisdom to the Lord, and he asked for more wisdom and discernment to rule his people. God increased the gift to meet the increased responsibility. "I will give you a wise and discerning heart, so that there will never have been anyone like you, nor will there ever be" (1 Kings 3:12). Solomon is known to this day for his wisdom. Unlike Daniel, we know that Solomon's commitment to God's way waned and he "loved many foreign women" (1 Kings 11:1). From then on his wise and prosperous rule declined. How sad.

If we are determined to follow the Lord and keep his ways, he will take our natural aptitudes and cause them to grow to outstanding gifts and even to supernatural proportions. What an opportunity!

Natural aptitudes and motivating skills are only one aspect of your personality. Together with your interests they add another piece to the jigsaw puzzle we are trying to build to give a picture of your unique personality. You should now have your data from the life patterns exercise listed under the seven headings. Keep these for your personal profile.

There is a second exercise you can do to help you identify your natural aptitudes. This is set out in appendix five. You may prefer to continue immediately with chapter five and return to appendix five later, when you are compiling your personal profile and you have a clearer idea if you want more data on natural aptitudes.

Talking Points

1. Ask each member of the group to relate one past achievement that they look back on with real pleasure, explaining what they did and how they went about doing it. In each case the other group members should try to discover what natural aptitudes they were using and what the motivation was behind the achievement.

2. See if you can ascribe a role or style to each member of the group. You may see one as an encourager, another as a helper and a third as an initiator. Recognizing each other's predominant role or style should improve the group's mutual appreciation of one another.

5

Values

• • •

*O*n the sixth day when God had finished creating the world, we are told that he "saw all that he had made, and it was very good" (Gen 1:31). God had a sense of accomplishment at having created something that was of value. He not only found satisfaction in the creation process, but he was satisfied with the result, with what he had achieved. What he had achieved was in harmony with what he valued. He is by nature Creator, and therefore produced "the created," and that creation was in harmony with what he is.

Our value system helps to determine just what we are going to enjoy doing. Values are a part of the jigsaw puzzle that makes up the satisfying, meaningful whole that gives us purpose in life. We get a sense of harmony when our activities are in line with our value system. If we are working out of phase with our value system, then we are like the bicycle wheel that is out of balance and that wobbles as we try to go faster.

After only a short acquaintance with someone I met recently, I could see that he was naturally gifted for the computer programming work that he did. He was an analytical thinker who loved "playing" with computers and working out computer programs. But he was deeply unhappy with his work and therefore with himself. Why? He was a a committed pacifist—and yet most of his work was for the Ministry of Defence in Britain. When he had finished creating the software (using all his natural gifts to the full) he was deeply disturbed because the results did not fit into his value system. It was not "very good" in his eyes. He saw all that he had made and to him it was very bad. Naturally he had no sense of accomplishment, as his work was out of harmony with who he was, with his deeply felt value system.

Our Emotional Paycheck

If values are the emotional paycheck of our work, some people are drawing no wages at all! We cannot expect to meet all of our expectations either in paid employment, in the church, in our hobbies or indeed anywhere. But even if our employment doesn't exactly fit our value system, perhaps we get deep emotional satisfaction in the home, seeing the family nurtured and growing up into caring, whole people. We can get deep satisfaction by being a functioning member of the local church. This is part of that for which we were created—to be a part of the body of Christ, helping to witness and care for God's people. We don't have to get satisfaction in every part of life, but we are in trouble if our work gives us no emotional wages, our home life is disordered and our spiritual lives are giving no reward.

Louis Raths and his colleagues, in their book *Values and Teaching,* define values as "those elements which show how a person has decided to use his life."[1] We may say that this is *why* we do things. Many missionaries and pastors work for less material reward than they would get in the secular job market, and yet a recent survey rated ministers as among those who are most satisfied with their work. Farmers also came high on the list, and undoubtedly growing crops and caring for animals fits in with many people's value system. "It is good!" as God said of his work. My own work puts me into contact with many missionaries who face difficulties and stresses and have low financial rewards—but few would change their work and, in spite of all the problems, most of them have a deep sense of satisfaction in what they are doing.

I am not, of course, suggesting that all Christians should be in so-called full-time Christian work, far from it! However, I feel deeply privileged to be able to work full time in something I find really satisfying and worthwhile.

Stephen Leacock said, "What we call creative work ought not to be called work at all, because it isn't. . . . I imagine that Thomas Edison never did a day's work in his last fifty years." The suggestion here is that Thomas Edison so enjoyed what he did that it shouldn't be called work. Edison valued his work. It appeared good to him.

Probably fewer people work for money than we imagine! People who retire often miss the sense of purpose and usefulness in what they were doing as much as they miss the cash. Human beings were created to work. Genesis 2:15 reads, "The LORD God took the man and put him in the Garden of Eden to work it and take care of it." No wonder farming comes out high on the list of most satisfying occupations!

Finding What We Value

How can we check on which values are involved in a particular task and how much satisfaction we are going to get from it? One way is by means of the list below of representative work values. Work values are those enduring dimensions or aspects of our work that we experience as important sources of satisfaction.

Promotion—opportunities to move ahead swiftly, gaining advancement and seniority

Adventure—risk-taking often involved in the work role

Challenge—demanding tasks or complex questions, problem solving or troubleshooting

Pressure—circumstances that demand fast-paced activity and work done rapidly

Proficiency—exercising competence, showing high level of effectiveness

Autonomy—being free to be independent and able to determine own activities

Influence—being in a position to affect or change other people's opinions

Academic Status—being acknowledged as intellectually able and scholarly

Originality—opportunity for free expression and creativity

Competition—opportunity to contend with others, striving to be the best

Variety—work content and setting that changes often

Service—helping other people directly, either practically or spiritually

Friendships—opportunities to develop close personal relationships at work

Material Gain—the likelihood of high earnings

Help Society—showing social responsibility, helping the community

Compatible Colleagues—working with those who share similar beliefs and values

Leadership—having the power to decide policies or courses of action and to be responsible for people

Stability—work that is predictable and not likely to change

Work Alone—working mostly without contact with others

Family—work that does not encroach on or upset family life

Security—work in which job tenure and long-term prospects and pension are good

Physical Challenge—needing to use bodily strength, speed or agility

Order—preferring to do one thing at a time

Work with Others—working with a close team of colleagues

Artistic Expression—expressing by writing, drama, painting, music and such

Self-growth—opportunities to make the most of self, to develop full potential

Prestige—gaining the respect of others because of job status

Research—work to expand frontiers of knowledge

Peaceful Atmosphere—lack of pressure

Spiritual and Moral Fulfillment—contributing to the achievement of spiritual and moral ideals

Balance—a well-adjusted lifestyle between work and the rest of life

Association—lots of opportunity for contact with people

Location—in the geographical place where you wish to live

Aesthetics—working in a pleasing environment and/or studying beautiful things

Values Card Sort

The list above includes thirty-four values. These values are set out in appendix six. If you feel you have any major values not covered, you may add them on the blank cards. You have two options for producing a set of "value" cards: you can photocopy them from the appendix and cut them up, or copy them by hand onto paper or note cards.

Now, take these cards and place them under the following five headings (make a 3″ × 5″ card for each heading) according to how important each value is to you.

Very Important	Important	Somewhat Important	Less Important	Least Important

When you have a pile of cards under each heading (they will not be even in number), rank each pile so that the most important are at the top under the head card, and the least important in that section are at the bottom. You can then record all this data on a values chart as follows. (Put the most important card in each of the five columns at the top of that column, and the least important in each of the five columns at the bottom of that column.)

Values Chart

Very Important	Important	Somewhat Important	Less Important	Least Important
_____	_____	_____	_____	_____
_____	_____	_____	_____	_____
_____	_____	_____	_____	_____

Keep this chart as part of your records.

You can now check these values against jobs you have done. List the eight values that you have rated most important. Use them to evaluate your work experiences in terms of how they allowed you to realize those values. If you have not had much work experience, then use tasks at school (such as being on the school magazine editorial staff), on a group holiday (such as being responsible for organizing the meals) and so forth. The following exercise should help you to determine what is important to you. Of the jobs you have done, consider the most satisfying, the least satisfying and the current one. Circle 1 to 5 depending on the degree to which you consider that value was met in that particular job (1 = not much to 5 = greatly). The total for each column will give a "score" for each job.

Your most important values	Your least satisfying job	Your most satisfying job	Your present job
1st	1 2 3 4 5	1 2 3 4 5	1 2 3 4 5
2nd	1 2 3 4 5	1 2 3 4 5	1 2 3 4 5
3rd	1 2 3 4 5	1 2 3 4 5	1 2 3 4 5
4th	1 2 3 4 5	1 2 3 4 5	1 2 3 4 5
5th	1 2 3 4 5	1 2 3 4 5	1 2 3 4 5
6th	1 2 3 4 5	1 2 3 4 5	1 2 3 4 5
7th	1 2 3 4 5	1 2 3 4 5	1 2 3 4 5
8th	1 2 3 4 5	1 2 3 4 5	1 2 3 4 5

Total

It is also important to look at those values that are least important to you. You can repeat the above exercise, listing your eight least important values and score 1-5 on the degree to which they are present in your most satisfying, least satisfying and present job. Obviously, a high score here indicates potential difficulty.

Now make yourself a values job review chart as follows and enter the totals for each of the six boxes.

Values Review Chart

	Least satisfying job	Most satisfying job	Present job
Eight most important values score			
Eight least important values score			

Jobs that are in harmony with your value system should read high against "Most important values" and low against "Least important values."

Since we are not always able to meet our needs adequately in paid employment, you may want to repeat the whole exercise against your present lifestyle and some past lifestyle or some projected future lifestyle. Lifestyle includes our job, church and recreational activity, and home/family life.

Values from Your Life Patterns Exercise

If you turn back to the life patterns exercise in the previous chapter, you should be able to identify what gave you satisfaction in each of the six achievements you described. Take these six "payoffs" and see if they throw any light on your value system. The values card sort is largely work values and the life patterns exercise looks at accomplishments in your wider life. However, the sense of satisfaction you gained in these six accomplishments should help you to identify your values.

For example, one of your accomplishments may have been to help an illiterate adult learn to read. At the end you may have described your satisfaction as, "I felt she was better prepared to face life." In this case we would expect to see "service" feature in your most important values.

Perhaps one of your accomplishments was to help in a local effort to clean up your town and free it of litter. You may have described your satisfaction as, "I felt our town was a nicer place to live in and people were more aware of the need to keep it clean." In this case we would expect to find "help society" among your most important values.

Values need not be such generally accepted values as the two examples above. Some other possible links are:

Accomplishment	Value
"I did it on my own."	Work alone
"I felt I had been a real friend."	Friendships
"I was the best."	Prestige
"Every day was different."	Variety

Christian Values

Values, perhaps more than any of the other facets of life we are attempting to measure, are affected by our Christian commitment. Our learning style, personality, interests and natural aptitudes are also affected by our faith, but to a lesser extent.

I recently did some work with a young man who was a lawyer. For some time he had been expressing dissatisfaction with his job. He had been for interviews with other companies and even considered leaving legal work and training in some other field. We looked at his interests, natural aptitudes, personality and several other factors. However, it was his value system that was out of harmony. He worked for a very large company where overheads and profit margins played a controlling factor in his daily work. He valued helping others. A satisfying day was when he felt that he had helped someone. He went back to his company and told them how he felt. As a company, they were moving toward larger and wealthier clients who could afford their high fees. To fit in with what he had told them, they began to give him all the cases of people in trouble who needed the sort of personal help that he wanted to give. He said that he was rushed off his feet! He also offered his services to a local group serving the disadvantaged, who could not afford to go to a lawyer. In this way he was fulfilling some of his value needs in his spare time.

The Christian should look at two possibilities:

1. Are my values correct? Are they in tune with God's value system as set out in his Word? How much of my value system is cultural, denominational and so on?

2. Is my lifestyle correct, or should I be altering my lifestyle to fit my values, which I believe are in line with God's values?

Are Our Values Correct?

First of all, where do we get our values from?

☐ some we are born with—temperament values

☐ some come from our environment—family values, cultural values

☐ some come from our faith—spiritual values

The Christian's value system must be a blend of these. We are not intended, even as Christians, to have one set of rigid values. Our values will change as we move through life. If, for example, we are dissatisfied with our day-to-day job because our main interest is in Christian work, then our energy, prayers and drive go into our church activities and we feel that life would be lovely if we could serve God full time. But we may need to alter our value system so that we see ordinary, everyday work as pleasing to God and part of his calling to us. I see many people who want to do more to serve God. This may be right. He may be calling them to a more direct role in Christian service. Perhaps, however, he wants them to see their secular job as his full-time service, to do it really well and shine for him there.

I believe that we need to examine our value system to see if our lifestyle is in harmony with it and then either modify one or the other so that we are not constantly dissatisfied with what we are doing. I meet Christians each year who say, "I'm not really sure that I am achieving very much (in my school, university, factory, office)." If you feel like this, either think through what God has called you to be so that you can serve him contentedly where you are, or move out to where you feel God would have you to be.

We have never had so much opportunity to change our lifestyle, and perhaps this is what brings dissatisfaction. When circumstances dictated that everyone should work "down the pit" or "on the farm" or "in service at the big house," they never questioned their lot. Now that we have educational opportunities, travel opportunities and far more job options, we have more of a difficult choice. What are we meant to be and do? For the Christian the options are even wider. As Christians we are not here just to fulfill ourselves, meet our needs, obtain our pleasures, but to ensure that our lives fulfill God's purposes. No wonder Christians often question whether they are in the right place or doing the right thing!

Biblical Characters

Joseph's career prospects in Potiphar's house were great. We are told that "the LORD was with Joseph and he prospered" (Gen 39:2) and that "Joseph found favor in his [Potiphar's] eyes and became his attendant. Potiphar put him in charge of his household, and he entrusted to his care everything he owned" (v. 4). After the trauma of his rejection by his brothers and being sold into slavery, Joseph was on the up and up. His abilities were recognized and he was getting satisfaction and fulfillment in using them.

When Potiphar's wife tried to seduce him, he refused, even though it meant loss of all that he had achieved. He knew that his values would be violated if he committed adultery and so he steadfastly refused. He was cast into prison and in the short term this meant a loss of status and the fulfillment and happiness he was getting in his job. However, God is faithful, and we know that he restored Joseph to even greater administrative responsibility.

Moses had many abilities suited to palace life. He had been brought up and educated in prestigious circles. We know that he had great abilities, as is demonstrated by his leadership of the people of Israel later in his life. The value of palace life was not as great to him as the value he placed on helping his people and serving his God. Instead of pursuing leadership in the palace, he identified with his own people. Initially we know this led to banishment to the land of Midian. His career prospects took a definite downward turn. Moses' integrity meant that he had to integrate his value system (my people, my God) into his life. Again, God honored Moses and raised him up to be one of the greatest men who ever lived.

Nehemiah also valued the honor of his God and was concerned for the plight of his people. He sat down and wept when he heard that "those who survived the exile and are back in the province [Judah] are in great trouble and disgrace. The wall of Jerusalem is broken down, and its gates have been burned with fire" (Neh 1:3). He risked his very high position in King Artaxerxes' household and administration to make his people's need known to the king.

He was possibly risking his life as well, in an era of despotic rulers. He said, "I was very much afraid" (Neh 2:2). He gave up his job (probably matching his skills and giving fulfillment) because his people's welfare and the honor of God's name were of greater value to him. He went out on a risky venture, vulnerable to those who were against his values, his people, his God. God sustained him and protected him and blessed his service. We see Nehemiah really using his administrative abilities for God in the rebuilding of the walls of Jerusalem.

Having done these exercises to determine your value system, we trust that you have a better "feel" for your value system and how it's operating in your life.

You should have for your personal profile: a values chart; a values job review chart; a list of "payoff" values.

Talking Points

1. Ask each person to name two or three values that are important to them and two or three that are of very little importance. Discuss how these values impinge on their everyday lives at work, at home and so forth.

2. Some values are negotiable; we can change them and may wish to do so if they hinder our lives and make us less able to function well. Some are less negotiable and are a part of the fabric of who we are. Missionaries often have to modify their values to match the host culture in which they serve. Discuss how we may need to change our values to reach the people around us with the good news and which values we cannot sacrifice to win others.

6

Personality Type

• • •

*B*ible characters stand out as clearly defined personalities, from melancholic Jeremiah to Nehemiah the man of action, from Paul the visionary leader to Moses the law-maker and leader. As we think of different Bible characters we associate certain characteristics with each one.

Exactly what personality is cannot be precisely defined, neither is it too clear from where we get it. However, we know that we are born with certain traits, inherited from our parents and forebears. We inherit both strengths and weaknesses. In addition, we are molded by our environment (culture, home life, life experiences). We can see God's hand in this, in that he is sovereign and knows all our circumstances (Ps 139:1-2). The time Moses spent in the palace in Egypt and in the desert at Midian prepared him for the task God had for him—to represent the people to Pharaoh and to lead them across the wilderness to the Promised Land.

Some people have used their personality to justify behavior that is not in accord with biblical teaching. Personality can never be used as an excuse to sin. Of course, each of us has strengths and weaknesses and we are likely to be tested in our weak areas. (The enemy seems to know us even when sometimes we do not know ourselves). Some of us are more prone to pride, some to anger and harsh words, others to laziness. Our personalities may explain why we fail in some ways and not in others, but they are not an excuse for sin.

Your personality manifests itself in the style or manner in which you interact with people or in which you approach activities. Your personality also affects how you handle and express your feelings and emotions. Some words that we use to describe personality include outgoing, meticulous, adaptable, gentle, warm, independent and so forth.

Personality Aspects in the Godhead

A delightful tenet of Scripture is that God made human beings in his own image (Gen 1:26). That an all-powerful Creator should seek to reflect himself in his creation, and particularly in humankind, is in itself a cause for wonder.

When we examine positive personality traits we can usually find these in the Godhead. When someone has a nurturing trait, seeks to care for others and help them grow, we know that the Lord is like this. When people are high in creativity we know that God himself is the source of creation.

In a personality indicator we shall be looking at later in this chapter, people are scored on a scale of how they view the world—from being very aware of present circumstances to being able to project their mind into the future. God does both of these with us. He meets people in their everyday lives and he is also the God to whom a day is as a thousand years, who sees the creation, the cross and the final passing away of this earth almost as one event. This is why many of the Old Testament prophecies speak to a particular circumstance (such as the nation of Israel at that time) as well as to future events.

Some of you have a preference for making judgments on a subjective basis. You consider mainly people values when making decisions. Others make judgments on a more factual basis, making decisions very objectively and logically. God did both together on the cross—the penalty for sin must be paid, justice must be done, yet "God so loved the world that he gave his one and only Son" (Jn 3:16). He felt deeply for humanity's plight and rescued them; at the same time upholding the logical, natural consequences of sin—that we should die.

God's nature is reflected in humankind, but each of us individually has only certain facets of his nature and even these are marred by sin. The New Testament reflects this in the teaching on the body of Christ in 1 Corinthians 12. One is the hand, another the foot, and so forth. Some people are carers, others thinkers, others . . . , but together we are more likely to reflect God to the world. Of course these very differences, instead of being a strength to God's people when they pull together, can be a weakness pulling us apart. Our sinful nature sees our own personality as the ideal and does not recognize that God is reflecting himself in a different way in others.

Personality Types

A very popular personality measure is the Myers Briggs Type Indicator.[1] This is increasingly being used for management purposes, in helping to develop teamwork and other interpersonal skills.

At the close of World War II Katharine Briggs and her daughter Isabel Myers wondered if there wasn't some way that people could live together more harmoniously and appreciate each other's differences rather than being in conflict so much. They developed a personality measure, based on the theory of Carl Jung, that yielded sixteen types—the Myers Briggs Type Indicator (hereafter referred to as the MBTI).

Gradually the indicator has grown in popularity and has been very widely researched and tested. It is used by educators and psychologists and is also used in Christian circles, particularly in missions where colleagues often have to work very closely together under trying and stressful conditions.

Courses on the MBTI are run by several secular agencies and also by those promoting its use among Christians. Some of these are listed in the Resources (appendix two), as are a number of books based on the work of Myers and Briggs.

We will look briefly at the four main parameters on which the Myers Briggs work is based and which are fairly fundamental, explaining the differences in human personality behavior.

It is important to realize that the MBTI measures *preferences,* not abilities. We each have a preferred style. This does not mean that we will *always* behave or react in certain ways. Some people are concerned that the theory of type puts people in boxes and somehow limits them. This is not so when it is used correctly, and indeed we shall seek to show that the opposite can be true. By discovering our preferred style and strengths, we can also recognize our weaknesses and seek to develop these.

The full indicator, published by Consulting Psychologists Press, needs professional scoring. Keirsey and Bates have a shorter temperament sorter in their book *Please Understand Me,* which you can score yourself.[2] (Details of both these and other publications on temperament and personality type and the MBTI can be found under Resources in appendix two.) The indicator yields a result that should give your preference in the following four continuums:

(I) Introversion _____ / _____ Extraversion (E)

Which is your preferred world of activity? Is it the inner world of ideas and concepts (Introversion) or the outer world of people and things (Extraversion)? The introvert is territorial and likes a reasonable degree of privacy. The extravert is much more sociable and is happy with a far greater degree of social interaction. An extravert may want to go to a party to relax whereas the introvert may need to escape from the party in order to relax. The extravert likes activity and uses "trial and error" methods. The introvert likes to think more deeply before taking action.

(S) Sensing _____ / _____ Intuition (N)

Which is your preferred way of perceiving information and data? Do you use your senses (eyes, ears, nose and so on) or your intuition? Sensing people usually notice details such as the color of people's eyes, what they wear and the like. They are down-to-earth, sensible, practical, in touch with reality and live very much for today. Those who have an intuitive preference easily forget names and details but see whole truths and concepts. Intuitives are speculative, inspirational and imaginative and often live in the future. The absent-minded professor is an extreme case of an intuitive. If the sensing people see the trees, the intuitives see the wood.

(T) Thinking _____ / _____ Feeling (F)

How we make judgments is the third continuum. Our preference can be to do this on the basis of impersonal logic, analysis and objectivity (Thinking) or on the basis of values, personal feelings and allowing for circumstances (Feeling). Those who prefer feeling judgments prize harmony and often are seen as warm and trusting individuals. Those who prefer thinking judgments often are seen as logical and firm and are more prone to skepticism.

(P) Perceiving _____ / _____ Judging (J)

The fourth continuum has to do with our preferred style of living.

Those with a judging preference like closure, that is, things settled and decided, while those with a perceiving preference like to keep matters open and undecided until all the data for a decision are available. Those with a perceiving preference live a more flexible and spontaneous lifestyle and may be described as fun-loving. Those with a judging preference live a more planned and regulated lifestyle and are work oriented.

You may wish to try to identify your type using the above descriptions of the four parameters. In each one, try to estimate which side is your preference. You should then have a code of four letters, such as INTJ. You can then check this against the descriptions of the sixteen types set out in the next section. Does the code you determined match the type description that you feel most closely describes you?

Do remember that you need to read further and take a professionally scored and validated indicator to get an accurate result as to your personality type according to the Myers Briggs Type Indicator.

The Sixteen Types

By indicating our preference on each of these four parameters using the initial letters—intuitive is designated by N to avoid confusion with introvert—we produce a four-letter code for each of the sixteen types.

INTJ—self-confident, decisive, pragmatic, brainstormers, analytical, independent, single-minded, theoretical . . . love challenges that require creative thinking, often rise to positions of responsibility, take organizational goals seriously . . . often found in scientific research, engineering and the like.

INTP—precise, logical, intellectual, diligent, reserved and impersonal . . . difficult to get to know, precise in thought and language, concentrate well, seek to understand the universe, often work alone . . . often specialize in philosophy, architecture, mathematics, university lecturing and so forth.

INFJ—complicated and complex, perfectionist, imaginative, vulnerable, warm, original . . . strong drive to help others, enjoy studying, high integrity, good interpersonal relations yet hard to get to know really well . . . often become psychiatrists, doctors, writers and so on.

INFP—loyal, idealistic, reticent, adaptable, honorable . . . facility with languages, welcome new ideas, avoid conflict, keep their word, not good decision-makers, profound sense of honor, like autonomy . . . often found in Christian ministry or missionary work, psychology and the like.

ENTJ—empirical, objective, dynamic, organized, hard working . . . can take hard decisions, intolerant of inefficiency, natural leaders, strongly driven to succeed, harness people to goals, expect a great deal from their spouses . . . often found in managerial positions, organizational leadership and so forth.

ENTP—ingenious, inspirational, resourceful, innovative, entrepreneurial . . . natural "people managers," like taking risks, respond well in crises, like to beat the system, rely on improvisation, natural conversationalists, like variety . . . make good management consultants, inventors and so on.

ENFJ—cooperative, influential, people oriented, socially adept, even tempered and tolerant, caring, trusting . . . can handle complex data, natural group leaders, know others' needs, may overextend themselves, can be idealistic in relationships, make devoted spouses, long for the ideal . . . make good actors/actresses, high-level salespeople, executives and the like.

ENFP—imaginative, ingenious, warmly enthusistic, credible, optimistic, charming, emotional, creative . . . sense the significance of events, very observant, easily bored, personalize work, good communicators, like freedom of action, poor on detail and follow-through . . . make good journalists, salespeople, play/screen writers and so forth.

ISTJ—serious, orderly, dependable, persevering, thorough, stable, faithful, unpretentious . . . support the status quo, keep the rules, their word is their bond, conserve resources, like consistent behavior in themselves and others . . . often found in banking, clerical, legal professions and so on.

ISTP—impulsive, fearless, egalitarian, flamboyant, cheerful, active . . . dislike obligations, thrive on excitement, easily bored, not good scholars, may ignore rules, keen on tools, poor verbal skills . . . make good artisans, drivers, laboratory technicians and the like.

ISFJ—responsible, dependable, hard working, loyal . . . primary desire to serve others, work is good and play must be earned, good homemakers, dislike supervising others, value traditions, relate best to those who need them, may take on too much . . . make good nurses, teachers, secretaries, middle managers and so forth.

ISFP—independent, sensitive, retiring, kind, sympathetic, optimistic, cheerful, modest . . . dislike arguments, live in the here and now, do not prepare and plan, value their hunches, keenly tuned senses, inclined to fine arts, love animals . . . found in a wide variety of occupations but especially gifted as dancers, painters, composers and so on.

ESTJ—punctual, responsible, matter-of-fact, consistent, dependable, neat, orderly . . . pillars of the community, outstanding organizers, enjoy traditions and rituals, may not be responsive to feelings and views of others, keep rules and expect others to . . . found in positions of responsibility in many fields as administrators.

ESTP—resourceful, sophisticated, active, witty, adventurous, charming, unpredictable, popular . . . good party people, seek excitement, make things happen, like the good life, live in the here and now, have lots of friends . . . make outstanding negotiators, troubleshooters, administrative firefighters, entrepreneurs and the like.

ESFJ—warm-hearted, talkative, orderly, conscientious, soft-hearted . . . most sociable of all types, harmony is treasured and worked for, supporters of home/school/church, excellent hosts, attend to the needs of others, need to be appreciated, expect others to follow the system, may be fearful . . . often in "people to people" jobs such as selling, preaching, teaching and so forth.

ESFP—optimistic, easygoing, generous, happy, adaptable, hedonistic . . . may be self-indulgent, attractive to others, low tolerance for anxiety, rely on personal experience, enjoy dramatic situations . . . often found in public relations, selling, the entertainment industry and so on.

What Does This Teach Us?

The main points to learn from personality type are:

1. I can accept my differences—I will not necessarily think and behave as others do.

2. I can accept that others will have different values and think of other things as important. They have a unique function as part of the body of Christ.

3. I can develop my preferences. For example, if I have an intuitive preference, I may not have allowed myself to use it to the full.

4. When I have developed my preferences and use them as fully as possible, I can develop the less-developed side of myself (the side of the continuums that I least prefer). If my preference is for thinking judgment I can develop my feeling judgment; if my perceiving preference is sensing I can develop my intuition. This is particularly so with the four functions, sensing/intuition and thinking/feeling—how we judge and how we perceive. *From Image to Likeness* by Harold Grant et al. discusses how we can develop our weaker preference.[3] This book was written in light of the use of the MBTI for over thirty years with Catholic missions.

5. Understanding types can also help my interpersonal skills in relating to others in the office, in the church and even in my marriage.

Doesn't this follow the biblical concept of parts of the body being different (see 1 Cor 12)? The eye, the ear, the nose are all so different, but they are all necessary for the healthy functioning of the body. We don't want to be all eyes, all ears, all noses. Overseas mission workers often live very closely together, more so than in our home culture. This means that we can find the differences in others irritating. In our home culture we are more able to escape from the situation! However, I have noticed over the years that friendships have formed between people who have not been able to escape from each other. They have gone on to appreciate the very differences that at first they found so irritating.

For example, I met a lady who attended one of our field training courses where new members live very closely with each other in simple living conditions for three months. By the end of this course one knows one's colleagues very well indeed! This person was middle-aged and this was her first experience of mission work and living in a Third World country. One year later she told me that she had made friendships in that course that she would not otherwise have made. Circumstances forced her to go beyond the kind of relationship with which she was comfortable, and she discovered that she could appreciate those she would normally find irritating and seek to avoid.

Teamwork

Teamwork is considered very important these days, and big companies are realizing that to stay ahead in the 1990s members of a work force must pull together harmoniously and not act competitively against each other. Departmental rivalry may have some positive aspects, but companies are more efficient when each department recognizes the value of the others.

Many years ago I worked for a company that produced complex cryogenic heat exchangers. There were plenty of interdepartmental tensions! The technical department designed the the machines to be as efficient as possible (but could they be made?); the production department wanted them designed so they were easy to make (but would they work and do their job efficiently?); the finance department wanted them produced cheaply (after all, we were in business to make a profit) . . . and so it went on. There were always interdepartmental clashes and frictions. The kind of remark often heard was "Just look what those idiots in the finance/

technical/production department have done now."

It's interesting that commerce and industry are now recognizing the need for us to value, rather than belittle, others whose skills and abilities differ from ours. The Bible clearly teaches that we each have different gifts and abilities and that we function best when we value God's gifts in others. The "body" teaching obviously is applicable to the church, but we can and do see that it also works in the secular world. It is pleasing when the secular world discovers a truth empirically, in this case that teamwork pays. It has been a part of Christian teaching for centuries.

Professor David Keirsey challenges us to "abandon the Pygmalion project, that endless attempt to change the other into a carbon copy of oneself." "It's O.K.," he says, "to marry your opposite and to have children who are far from being chips off the old block, but it's not O.K. to take marriage and parenting as license to sculpt spouse and child using yourself as a pattern to copy. *Put down your chisel. Let be. Appreciate.*"[4]

Personality in the Bible

How would you describe Paul's personality characteristics? Was he mild and humble, quiet and self-effacing? That's not the picture I get when I read Acts and the Pauline epistles. Assertive, bold, great visionary, thinker and scholar are a few words that come to mind. I am not sure I would have found him easy to live with. He doesn't appear to have suffered fools gladly.

What about Peter? How would you describe him? I see him as impulsive, enthusiastic, sociable, a leader, to name a few. I think I would have found it easier to relate to Peter, but God used both him and Paul mightily. They were his servants. As their lives were yielded to him, God took them and used their personality strengths to further his kingdom.

Corporate Ethos

So far we have considered individual identity and personality. Is there such a thing as corporate identity? Can we see specific personality traits in groups of people? Modern management is beginning to pay increasing attention to the "company ethos." Each company has one or more characteristics that identify it and distinguish it from others. For some companies "quality" is their keynote, for others "efficiency," and for others "lowest prices."

People joining these companies are usually given some induction or training to help them become aware of the company ethos and value system. Sometimes that ethos has to be reinforced so that the workforce all has the same vision and work to the same end. At other times the ethos needs to be modified or altered to suit a changing world. A merger means adaptation on the part of both companies and their employees. A takeover can be very threatening to the employees of the company being taken over.

Missionary societies also have a corporate identity. They are very different from each other even when their aims are the same. I often say to potential candidates that they need to make sure that the mission they join is one in which they can feel at home and in which they feel they can fit. One Canadian man, very extraverted, very artistic and individualistic, came to work in an overseas mission's home office in Britain. The home office of a mission, with its emphasis on finances and procedures, is often more conservative than an overseas branch. His reaction was, "Am I peculiar or are they peculiar?" The answer is neither—just different.

When we move to a new situation, it helps if we recognize that the company ethos (or the new subculture) may be different. This may threaten us and challenge our values and expectations, and we need time and patience to adjust.

Do denominations have a corporate identity? Do individual churches have a distinct personality? Most certainly! I can think of three churches with which I have been associated, and each has its own individuality. I appreciate all three and can see variety and strengths in these differences, just as there are with different people.

One church runs very much to time and order. Services are scheduled. If you take part you know when, where and for how long. Another is much more spontaneous. Things are left vague and loose and arranged either just before the service or even impromptu, while the service is in progress. One church has a preference for structure and order and the other for spontaneity and a relaxed and free atmosphere. In settling in a new church it is good to recognize this difference. Equally, when a new leader is appointed, he or she will tend to bring a distinctive personal style. This takes adjustment on all sides and can produce friction.

Do certain personalities join certain types of churches? I would love to do some research and see whether there is a significant correlation between personality type and church denominations. I suspect that the results may shake a few theological assumptions!

There are no results of tests or measures to keep for your personal profile from this chapter. However, as we have considered personality and looked at one indicator, you may be able to write a brief description of your main characteristics. You could write a sentence about how you relate to others—gregarious, shy, friendly and so forth. Another sentence could describe your attitude toward work—conscientious, prefer to have a "boss" to check with, like lots of challenge and the like. A third sentence could describe how you handle and express your feelings and emotions—reserved, high-strung, calm, relaxed and so on. Keep this description in your folder to help you compile your personal profile.

Talking Points

1. Where do we get our personality from? Are we born with it, inheriting it with our genes, or is it the result of being molded by our environment? How is God at work in each of these? Can we change our personality or are we stuck with it for life?

2. Ask the group members to name two personality characteristics that they feel they possess (shy, assertive, high achiever, forthright and so on).

In each case discuss how these can be a strength or a weakness to the person concerned and to the group as a whole.

3. Discuss the concept of our strengths being our weaknesses and our weaknesses being our strengths.

4. Are some personality characteristics more "Christian" than others? For example, some people seem to be naturally "good," wanting to follow and keep to the rules. Others seem rebellious by nature, always challenging the status quo. What can we do about this? Are these different characteristics equally O.K.?

5. Does God have a personality? See if you can identify the attributes of the Godhead (loving-kindness, justice, holiness, creativity and so forth). We are made in his image. Do we find these attributes in people?

6. Can you identify the corporate identity of your church or group? Does this explain why some have found it harder to fit in than others? Is this corporate identity a help or a hindrance in reaching the people of your neighborhood?

7

Learning
Style

• • •

*P*eople learn in different ways. Our educational system doesn't always allow for this and hence some of you may see yourselves as "not very clever," "not very academic" or even "not very good at anything." You may be underestimating yourself simply because of some negative educational experiences. I once asked someone with whom I was doing career counseling what she was good at. She thought for a few minutes and then said, "Nothing." In fact she was quite good at many things, but the education she had received in no way matched her preferred style of learning—and so she felt she couldn't learn.

Differences in learning style depend on many things: our temperament, how we have been taught, our family background and upbringing, our perception of ourselves, and others' expectations of us. Researchers believe that two major parameters determine how we learn. The first is how we perceive—that is, how we take in information. The second is how we process that information—that is, what we do with it.

How We Perceive

People perceive reality differently. We look at the same situation but we see different things. If two people walk into a cathedral, one's impression may be the cost of building it, how long it took to build and what construction method they used to get such huge pieces of masonry up to such a height. The other may be awed by the architectural beauty, a sense of God's presence and a sense of being a part of history. If these two people wrote a report on what they saw, we might wonder if they had visited the same place! There are many facets to how we perceive, but a simple way to represent this parameter is with a diagram.

Concrete
|
|
|
|
|
Abstract

Those who perceive "concretely" are likely to learn more through experience. They immerse themselves in reality rather than in abstract thinking. They like "hands-on learning" to take in information. They tend toward subjectivity. They are *sensors/feelers*.

Those who perceive the world in an abstract way are inclined to analyze and think through the information received; their intellect makes the first appraisal. They are rational and logical and tend toward objectivity. They are *thinkers*.

How We Process Information

This parameter is simply represented by another diagram.

Active — — — — — — — — Reflective

Active processors like to get on and use the information or experience they have perceived. They are *doers*.

Reflective processors like to mull over the experience or information they have received and see how it fits in with the existing bank of information they have stored (what they know), and work out how it fits in with their scheme of things. They are *watchers*. Both ways of perceiving are valid and valuable.

Since there are two major aspects to learning style (how we perceive and how we process information) and since—in our simple scheme—each of these aspects can be approached in two ways, we can divide the learning process into four segments.

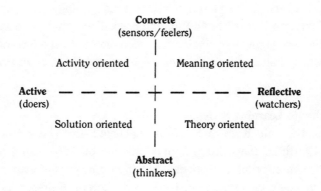

This way of looking at how we learn gives us four types of learning style: meaning oriented, theory oriented, solution oriented and activity oriented. None of us is a pure type; we all use some of each type, but most of us have a preferred style or combination of types that we use in learning.

Other Learning Style Categorizations

An alternative way of looking at our learning style is to contrast the linear learner with the global learner. The linear learner is the abstract thinker, who has a preference for analytical reasoning. He or she prefers to see the small parts that make up the whole before trying to understand the whole. This approximates to the theory-oriented and solution-oriented types.

The global learner, sometimes called the holistic learner, prefers to grasp the whole picture at once. This approximates to the meaning-oriented and activity-oriented types. Such a person prefers to see the whole picture and then to understand later the parts that make up the whole. This two-way split is, of course, simpler to handle but uses only the perceiving parameter and ignores the processing parameter.

There are several other ways of categorizing learning styles. One which has received prominence in recent years is left brain versus right brain thinking preference. People often use this terminology along with the false assumption that left brain thinking is good and right brain thinking is bad. The left brain/right brain idea approximates to the linear/global dimension. I shall be using the linear/global and the four-way categorization.

Research into Learning Styles

There has been much research into how people learn. The four-way pattern, put forth by David Kolb, is only one way of representing how we learn.[1] It is interesting that others, studying from very different perspectives, have come up with a similar four-way pattern. Keirsey and Bates, in their book on personality types, suggest four learning styles allied to four basic temperaments. The Resources section lists some references for those who wish to read further.

Bernice McCarthy, in her book *The 4 MAT System,* has compared all these different research results and attempted to show their similarity.[2] She also suggests that we should all try to learn in a cycle using all four styles. We start by experiencing—sensing and touching. We then go on to reflect on this data and to analyze the information, fitting it into our existing knowledge and understanding of how things work. We then apply this knowledge by doing and experimenting. Finally, we begin gathering new data and repeat the cycle.

Learning Style and You

Just as you have a uniquely created personality, so you have your own individual preferred learning style. It will have similarities with some other people's learning style and can be compared with the learning style types listed above, just as your unique personality can be compared with other people's personality types. We can determine our preferred style, the way we learn best, and compare it with the way others learn.

Different situations demand the application of different learning styles, but that does not negate the fact that we each have a preferred learning style. As you consider your individual learning style you will find food for thought about how you experienced (or experience) school, how you teach (in church, for example) and how to make good choices about any further study that you hope to do.

The learning type test in appendix seven should help you to determine your preferred style. Turn to it now and do the test before I explain more about the types, as this may bias your responses to the test. Note that the results will not exactly match those from other learning style tests.

Interpreting Your Result

Your result from the learning type test is not definitive. To validate your result simply read the four type descriptions below and decide how much of each type you use when you learn. Award yourself a score out of ten for each type description and multiply this score by four. You can then compare this result with your result from the inventory.

Meaning-Oriented Learners

These people gather data concretely and process it reflectively. They use their senses well in observing life and tend to sit back and consider what they have observed. They value harmony, personal involvement and commitment. They spend their lives trying to find their true identity and become a complete individual. Their focus is on people. Their favorite question is "Why?"

When learning they value personal relationships with the teacher and with other students. They like to work together in a cooperating group and not in a competitive environment. Meaning is important to them and they need to know the relevance of what they learn. They empathize with those who fail even when they themselves succeed, and they will want to stop and help the slower student at the expense of their own progress. They learn from discussion, role-play and drama. The classroom atmosphere should be democratic. Where these needs are not met we find the unhappy student who comes home at night to pour out his or her woes.

Recognition: Meaning-oriented learners need positive feedback and affirmation. Negative criticism and conflict are counterproductive to learning. They take very seriously and personally evaluations of their work. They see them as a measure of themselves.

When teaching others meaning-oriented learners expect their students to think things through—to watch and observe and carefully examine the data. As they are interested in their own self-growth, so they are interested in the growth of others. They are as interested in helping a not very bright person to take a few steps forward as in helping a "straight-A" student. They seek good relationships with their students and may use a tutorial system. Their teaching role is facilitator.

People with this learning preference are often found among social scientists, counselors, tutors, musicians, historians, artists and so forth. Many of them choose professions that serve others: nursing, teaching, medicine or full-time Christian service.

Theory-Oriented Learners

These people gather data abstractly and process it reflectively. They begin with a concept or an idea, and then think around it. They use their minds well and think with logical precision and value sequential thinking. They value intellectual competence and like to know what the experts think. They're impatient with subjective judgment. Facts are more important than feelings, and theirs is a constant quest for knowledge. Their danger is that they spend too much time in the ivory tower. Their favorite question is "What?"

When learning they are comfortable with a factual and analytical style of teaching. They are independent learners, and if their quest for knowledge is not met they may be off "doing their own thing." They can underachieve if not stimulated sufficiently. They will follow up classroom work with their own reading and/or research. They may be seen as cold and not having sufficiently developed social skills. They tend to interact only with the teacher and with other "bright" students, whom they see as their intellectual equals. They may see recreation and social activities as a waste of time.

Recognition: Theory-oriented learners need to succeed, since competence is of very high value to them. Failure can be devastating, and yet they set higher and higher standards for themselves. They can accept criticism from those they view as competent, providing they can see the validity of it. Justice is important to them, and they take it very hard if they feel they are treated unjustly. They will examine their evaluations to check their accuracy!

When teaching others their basic aim is to transmit knowledge and to share their own love of knowledge. They do this by presenting the information in a systematic and orderly fashion that should fit in with the students' existing theoretical framework. There will be lots of facts and data. They will enjoy the outstanding student but may get frustrated with the slow student. In the classroom they are fair but authoritative.

People with this learning preference are often found among researchers, scientists and mathematicians. They tend to choose careers where logical thought is required.

Solution-Oriented Learners

These people gather data abstractly and process it actively. They start with a concept or idea, and then seek to try it out and see if it works, integrating theory and practice. Their danger is that they leave the ivory tower too soon, not having thought everything through sufficiently. They enjoy finding practical solutions to problems. They value common sense and pragmatism. They are oriented to support their school, company or organization. They are reliable people to whom duty and service are important. Their favorite question is "How does this work?" Their focus is on results.

When learning they like structure and clear instructions concerning what is expected of them. They feel at home in the traditional classroom and seek to please the teacher. They try to do all set work but are not so happy with unsupervised projects. These students usually enjoy school. They like learning facts but are uneasy when required to exercise ingenuity and imagination.

Recognition: Solution-oriented learners respect the teacher and therefore take the teacher's comments seriously. If criticized they respond with more effort. These students, more than any other type, respond to evaluations.

When teaching others the aims of solution-oriented learners are utilitarian: to give the training needed to do the job or to prepare the students for life. Their focus is on the end product. They expect productivity and hard work from their students. These teachers are the closest to the traditional teaching model, particularly in classroom management. There may be plenty of practical, hands-on activity, providing this fits the subject matter. They will back up the information they present by showing that it works rather than by extensive theoretical proof.

People with this learning preference are often found among engineers, applied scientists such as metallurgists, zoologists, botanists, environmental scientists and food technologists, and other practical technicians.

Activity-Oriented Learners

These people gather information concretely and process it actively. They use their senses well in experiencing life and apply this information to the practical world around them. Their strength is their flexibility and their ability to move out into the world and achieve results. They like freedom to act and can be fun-loving and adventurous.

When learning they enjoy plenty of physical involvement and hands-on experience. Verbal and visual work are more helpful to them than pen and paper work. They learn well when there is plenty of variety and new material, and conversely are not stimulated by routine and detail. They enjoy extracurricular activities and the communal aspects of school life.

Recognition: Activity-oriented learners like to be on good terms with the teacher (although they are not as sensitive as the meaning-oriented people). If their classroom needs are not met they may try to change the system or opt out and get on with their own thing. Of all the types they are the least concerned with evaluations.

When teaching others these learners encourage experiential learning, and their classrooms have a creative atmosphere with plenty of variety. They like to get alongside their students and help them achieve their own objectives. They may not keep to the curriculum. They motivate by their enthusiasm and are themselves motivated by improving the community.

People with this learning preference are often found in the entertainment world, in marketing and sales, among businesspeople and in the social professions. Some go into teaching, particularly with younger children and/or less academically inclined students.

Some Hypothetical Results

You can ascertain the degree to which you use each type by taking the test in appendix seven and/or by matching yourself to the above type descriptions. Your individual learning style is how you prefer to use the four types. Some people have a marked preference for one type while others use two, three or even all four. Let's look at some possible results to give you some examples of how you may go about interpreting yours.

Bias to One Type. Let's assume a result showing a marked preference for one type, theory oriented. Out of forty, we get scores of meaning oriented, 22; theory oriented, 38; solution oriented, 15; activity oriented, 16.

A person with a result like this is a highly analytical learner. It is very important that any new data this type of learner receives is fitted into the framework of his or her existing knowledge. This person may be described as academic and intellectual, and may appear clinical and logical. He or she does not like subjective judgments but enjoys scientific subjects and dealing with facts.

No Bias. Let's assume a result showing a fairly even use of all four types: meaning oriented, 24; theory oriented, 28; solution oriented, 30; activity oriented, 27.

A person with a result like this is able to take in information both by experiencing and by abstract concepts. He is able to reflect on the information and go ahead and use it. Such a person can make a good teacher. He should be able to adapt easily to using the teaching/learning style for the situation. However, because he can use strategies from all the learning types, as a teacher he may not understand a person whose learning style is one pure type and does not have the option to easily adopt a different approach to learning.

Bias to Two Types. Let's assume a result showing a preference for two types: meaning oriented, 38; theory oriented, 18; solution oriented, 22; activity oriented, 37.

This result shows the person to be a strongly global learner. He or she has a strong preference for gathering information by experience. This learner prefers practical subjects to theoretical ones, but is able equally to reflect on the information and to make practical use of it. He or she likes learning by participation in groups and learns best in a harmonious, noncompetitive environment. He or she prefers a good relationship with the teacher.

Understanding Ourselves

How can we use this knowledge of our learning style? What practical applications has it, or is it just theory?

If your learning style is predominantly theory oriented, that is, you gather information abstractly and then process it reflectively, then you are a thinker/watcher, and you probably found that our schooling system suited you and you obtained, or are obtaining, benefit from it. Our educational system increased your self-confidence since you probably did well.

If your learning type is solution oriented, then again you were probably able to "succeed" at school, but you are probably bored by study as such and only do so where you can see the purpose. Meaning-oriented and activity-oriented types probably enjoy academic learning least.

Of course, you may have been taught more holistically or globally, and benefited from that. Also, some global and holistic learners are so academically bright that they succeed in spite of the teaching system. Some go on to advanced study, although usually in nonanalytical subjects.

By knowing your learning style you can sometimes make sense of your history—why you succeeded here and why you had more difficulty there. As in the case of the lady I mentioned earlier, who thought of herself as not very bright or clever, you may be able to reassess yourself.

You should be able to see why you found certain subjects easier than others. Analytical learners enjoy mathematics and science, and indeed any subject that seeks to understand the world in which we live. Perhaps you were best at the practical (concrete experience) subjects such as wood-work or domestic crafts and you now see that you learn better through hands-on experience.

It helps most of us to stop comparing ourselves unfavorably with others who are different from us and start accepting ourselves as who we are. God has not made a mistake. Even our preferred learning style is a part of his design.

Understanding Others

I recently spent some time with a colleague whose daughter was not happy at school; she was not getting good results—particularly in the frequent tests and exams. The situation had deteriorated with a recent change of classroom teacher. Her younger brother loved school, and un-fortunately she was comparing herself unfavorably with him. She received a lot of love and support from her family, but her mother was concerned that she was developing a "complex" about not being "any good" and, in particular, about always feeling second best compared with her brother.

Fortunately, her mother understood her well, and the little girl talked frequently to her about how she felt about school. As the mother shared these things with me, it was clear that the child's preferred learning style included many of the aspects of a global learner. Some tests, which the mother did vicariously on behalf of the child, confirmed this. She enjoyed group processes and working together; a happy atmosphere; a warm teacher-pupil relationship; descriptive subjects. She did not enjoy analyt-ical subjects or exams and tests, where she did worse than in classwork.

The mother went to see the teacher, who agreed to try to do all she could to make the girl's learning environment as near her preferred style as possible. There seemed to be real improvement. In addition, the child benefited as she saw that her style was different and neither better nor worse than other children's. She (or her mother) could seek to change what was changeable, and modify and supplement what they could not alter. Some extra teaching to supplement the analytical teaching—giving it purpose and meaning, explaining the breadth of the subject matter and where it was leading—was of help. As the little girl understood and accepted herself, she began to avoid the pitfall of labeling herself "not clever."

Thinking about learning styles enables us to understand others better—and to help them.

Modifying Our Learning Styles

As Bernice McCarthy indicates, perhaps we should learn using all four models. We need to sense and feel (experience) and then to cogitate and reflect on what we have experienced. Then we think and theorize. Then we apply what we have learned by experimenting. Then we start the process again by building on this first cycle of knowledge.

You are unlikely to find a perfect learning situation, and indeed each subject requires a different balance of the four styles. In learning how to change a baby's diaper you might not feel it appropriate if you were taught the theory of how one way of folding a cloth diaper distributes the forces of the restraining pins differently from another! You would want to have a go yourself and learn by active participation.

It is a mistake to assume that you are stuck with one learning style and can never effectively learn any other way. You may always have your own preferred style, comprising one or more types, but you can learn to use and benefit from other types. If you are in a situation where one type is used, and it doesn't suit you, then you can supplement this by teaching yourself by using other types, in your spare time.

The practical course can be modified by reading and understanding the theory. The theoretical course can be supplemented by getting some hands-on experience. You can try to supplement the parts of the learning cycle you are not getting, particularly those parts that are important to you.

You sometimes have a choice of training paths, and it can help you to know how these various options are taught. For many years some local schools have sought to teach more globally. Some courses at college level have a much greater practical, hands-on element than others. Even in subjects like medicine some medical schools involve their students with real patients at a much earlier stage than others, and some almost from the beginning. It seems common sense that, if you understand your own learning style, you can try to plan your future training to take this into account.

Being More Effective in Teaching Others

In our Wycliffe linguistic training in Britain we now run two streams, one for predominantly linear learners and another for more global learners. Linguistics is an analytical subject and traditionally has been taught that way, but since the introduction of the global stream, a lot of people who might otherwise have struggled through without really getting to grips with the subject have benefited from the training.

I recently attended one of our field training courses, helping to prepare translators for living in rural Africa. In this particular course the formal lectures were reduced to a minimum. The course was globally taught, the object being to help the participants enjoy some real-life experience of rural Africa. It proved to be a positive, enjoyable learning experience.

A local mission doctor asked the training course director if the participants could help in an immunization program for the village children. Some gave injections, others held the children, some kept the records. Everyone was there and participating. The doctor had given a lecture on injections and taught the participants how to give them. He also came back to the course after the program and taught more health theory and explained how the tetanus, measles, typhoid and TB injections would help the people. He gave statistics of the present incidence of these health problems, including the mortality rate. The learning process included giving the injections, holding the trembling children and seeing the differing reactions of the local people to the children's fear. This taught so much more than lectures alone could ever do, making it a really good learning experience.

Think about any teaching you are involved in. Could you modify your approach so that it matches others' learning styles—or picks up on all four in a "learning cycle"?

Learning and the Christian

One phrase that occurs again and again in Scripture is: "so that you may know." God is very interested in teaching us and helping us to grow and learn. Sometimes it says "to teach you" or "then you will know," but the thrust is the same. God allows events to happen to people—individuals and nations—to teach them and train them in the way that they should go.

There seem to be few classrooms in the Scriptures. This is, of course, mainly a cultural phenomenon, but nevertheless it is true that in the Bible the emphasis is on learning through experience. The Bible is full of examples of God teaching people through experience. When the Israelites arrived at the Red Sea, God could have had the way open, ready for them to cross. But he wanted them to stop, with the barrier of water ahead and the dust of Pharaoh's chariots on the horizon behind. "Help, what can we do?" How many of us have been in impossible situations brought about by God so that he can teach us that he is our deliverer?

Similarly, God provided for the Israelites' physical needs in the wilderness. Deuteronomy 8:3 says, "He humbled you, causing you to hunger and then feeding you with manna, which neither you nor your fathers had known, *to teach you* that man does not live on bread alone but on every word that comes from the mouth of the LORD."

When they reached the Promised Land, Joshua said, *"This is how you will know* that the living God is among you and that he will certainly drive out before you the Canaanites, Hittites, Hivites, Perizzites" (Josh 3:10). In this case God divided the waters of the Jordan to show his power and to give them faith to believe that he would overcome the inhabitants of the land and drive them out.

Elijah on Mount Carmel said to the Lord, "Answer me, so these people *will know"* (1 Kings 18:37). Joel 2:27, referring to the rains coming and to floors full of wheat, says, "Then you *will know* that I am in Israel."

We find that Jesus' teaching style is similar to that seen in the Old Testament: he uses experience to teach. He said, before healing the paralytic, that he was doing this *"so that you may know* that the Son of Man has authority" (Mt 9:6).

God seeks to demonstrate to an unbelieving world that he sent Jesus and that he loves the world, through a living lesson in the unity of believers. In John 17:23 Jesus prayed, "May they be brought to complete unity *to let the world know* that you sent me and have loved them even as you have loved me."

There are many, many more examples, both in the Old Testament and in the New Testament, of God encouraging people to learn through life experiences.

Teaching the Christian Faith

As we have seen, the bulk of our training and teaching is conducted in a linear (or analytical) manner, whereas it is now believed that the majority of people are global or holistic learners. One of the problems with the teaching in our churches is that much of it is analytical. The church has attracted middle-class, often university-educated, analytical learners. These people usually rise to positions of leadership, and the clergy also often come from their ranks.

Jesus taught his disciples in the school of experience. He had them with him most of the time, showing them by his actions as well as his words the will of the Father. He commissioned them and sent them out (both the Twelve and the seventy) to go and *put into practice* what he had been showing them. They worked with Jesus (experiencing), reflected on what he did, fitted it into their existing knowledge of God, and then went out and did these things themselves. Note how close this is to the researchers' experience of a balanced learning style.

There seems to be very little explanation of the spiritual order of things in the Scriptures. There is almost no systematic theology laid out for us. We have to glean it by reading what happened and what Jesus and others said when they spoke about real-life experiences. This is not to say that analytical learning or teaching is wrong, but that we must be careful that we don't ignore or even invalidate global/holistic, practical, hands-on experiential learning. I wonder how much of our learning in the local church contains all four aspects of the learning cycle? I sense that Jesus gave his disciples a broad-based learning experience as they traveled about Galilee with him.

For many years, evangelical teaching had a heavy bias toward the theoretical. It was considered important that people should "understand" and "know" the way of salvation. Feelings were suspect. Theory is not bad—in fact it's true—but it is not the whole truth.

The charismatic renewal movement has somewhat redressed this balance. In some cases it may be too feeling and experience orientated and need the balance pushed back the other way. Nevertheless, Christians in the pew are participating more and experiencing their faith more today than they were, in my experience, in the 1950s and 1960s. One of the criticisms leveled at the renewal movement is that it is too experiential. This undoubtedly has some truth in it, and too many folk in the renewal movement seem to be constantly "sensing" and "feeling" what God is saying to the exclusion of understanding God's word and his commands, which stand forever no matter what we feel. On the other hand, the renewal movement has begun to reach people who were largely untouched by more traditional evangelical orthodoxy, which relies more on the mind. Both are valid and both are necessary.

Experiencing the Gospel

I meet many people who have become Christians because they could see and experience the Christian gospel in action, whether it was through a worship style where they could feel God's power and presence, or whether God entered into the everyday events of their lives. The minister at our local church teaches in a very global style. He has a warm, caring approach in his teaching. He tends to go around his subject many times during the course of a sermon, increasing the scope of the circle of knowledge being taught each time. He does not usually seem to analyze the subject.

I confess that with a science degree and a theological diploma, I have found him difficult to follow and wished he would put his teaching more systematically. But surely it is more important that the majority—particularly those young in the faith—learn, than that the presentation should suit someone of my background. Needless to say, I have learned a lot over the years as I have appreciated this different style. I have met many people who have said how much they have learned under his ministry. New Christians have been encouraged to "get involved" from the beginning, rather than waiting until they are experienced Christians. This also has helped them to grow and learn.

With possibly two-thirds of the population being global learners, we need more global teachers of the gospel. We are all involved in some way in the business of teaching and discipling others. We need to pay attention to the way people, and adults in particular, learn. Let us seek to be as effective as possible in teaching others. This means remembering that most people are not linear learners.

Knowing God

The word *know* implies one's whole being—those parts of us affected by what we have experienced as well as the intellect. Our character and personality are modified by our life experiences; God causes growth in our lives by the things that we experience as well as by what we learn in books and sermons.

The Bible talks about wisdom, the knowledge and understanding of God, but I believe we can also understand that wisdom to include the knowledge of the natural world around us. The latter without the former is pointless to the Christian. When we know God we have all knowledge.

Modern men and women have largely abandoned knowing God and have sought instead to know and understand his universe, the natural world around us. The Christian seeks to know both, with the primary emphasis on knowing God.

You should keep your learning type test result so that you can incorporate it in your personal profile.

Talking Points

1. Ask each member of the group to identify their preferred learning style. Discuss different educational histories and how each person's learning style has been affected by this.

2. Try to identify the teaching styles used in your youth group, in your Sunday school, in your church services, and so forth. How do these fit the needs of the congregation and the people of the area you serve?

3. Discuss how God has taught you. Perhaps you have been most helped by a good Bible teacher, or perhaps a more experienced Christian "discipled" you. Is God teaching you through life's experiences? Does God find it difficult to teach you or are you open to his input into your life?

8
Life
Changes

• • •

C hange is a part of life. We may sometimes wish that we could stop the clock, that life would stand still, that we need not age. However, this is not possible. The only person who does not change or grow old is the Lord. It is very reassuring, in the midst of a lot of change, to meditate on the one who said, "I the LORD do not change" (Mal 3:6).

The positive side of the inevitability of change is that change can be part of the growth process. It used to be thought that our capacity for learning faded away once we reach adulthood. We now know that this is not so. The good news is that we can go on learning and growing right into old age. In Canada, a major study of adult learning projects found that nearly 70 percent of the projects surveyed were self-planned.[1] That is, people were the instigators of change and growth in their own lives. I think we must all have areas in our lives in which we want to change, or in which we are aware that the Lord wants to change us. And change is possible.

Lifelong Learning

The possibility of lifelong learning and change and growth is a liberating thought, and I believe it is biblical. Abraham is a good example. He was seventy-five years old before he even left Haran and set out for Canaan. He was one hundred before he became the father of Isaac. The Bible records much change, growth and new revelation to Abraham in the intervening period, and Abraham's growth does not stop there either. Another example is Moses, who was eighty years old before he accepted the task of leading the people of Israel out of captivity. Consider Joseph, Daniel or Paul—the Bible is full of examples of God at work throughout people's lives.

The book of Proverbs contrasts young men, eager to make their mark in life, with fathers and mothers whose role is to correct and guide the younger generation. The Bible sees old people as those who have gained wisdom in their passage through life and can pass that wisdom on to others. Titus 2 gives instructions for teaching older men and women so that they can guide younger men and women.

The observation of identifiable phases in people's lives goes back at least as far as Shakespeare. He wrote about the seven stages of life in *As You Like It*. Research into life-phase identification began in the 1920s. Researchers agree that there are phases in people's lives and that these can be identified as common in general to a given age group. How many these phases are and at approximately what age each is reached seems more problematic. Chronological age is definitely only to be considered as a rough guide.

Some consider the role of age to be crucial in determining life phase. Others believe it is social role, such as being a student, newlywed, middle-aged parent and so forth, which is really the determining factor. Each phase of life has its own specific tasks. Which phase you are now in, or about to enter, must obviously have a marked effect on your lifestyle, career plans, family commitments, church involvement and the like. How you will express and use the gifts God has given you must vary according to where you are in your life cycle.

Your Life Cycle

Where are you in your life cycle? I do not propose to consider the phases of childhood and adolescence, but to start at the beginning of adulthood. Obviously not all of us will fit exactly into the generally accepted phases, but I think you will find it helpful to consider where you are now and the effect this may have on your present and future roles and tasks. If you are between about eighteen and twenty-three years of age, some of the tasks that you are probably engaged in include establishing your own autonomy and independence from your family, defining who you really are, and making new adult friendships with your own peer group. You may be leaving home, entering college or choosing a spouse. All of these tasks inevitably influence your choices—of career, leisure occupations, where you live and so on.

If you are in your mid to late twenties, your tasks include developing the capacity for intimacy, which may be expressed by getting married or establishing close friendships. Another task is to plan your life structure. Another may be becoming a parent. Your career and other choices are influenced by these tasks. You may need to establish a home suitable for children, earn enough money to support a family, and so forth.

Those of you who are in your early thirties and married may see staying put in one location for the family's sake and establishing your children in various schools as some of your tasks for now. At this stage in life such tasks as striving for success, searching for stability, security and control may also be important. If you are single, the right career path may be even more significant for you than for those who are married.

In your late thirties and early forties, for some of you a "midlife crisis" age has arrived. Some typical tasks include facing the reality of aging and mortality. It is a time when you may be reassessing your marriage and your personal priorities and values. Some typical events are crucial promotion and responsibility for aging parents as well as for growing children. For many married women, this is the beginning of the empty nest and a time to consider reentering a career or taking up further educational opportunities. Many do both of these.

From the "midlife crisis" stage we enter middle age. If you are in this phase of life, some of your tasks are to increase your feelings of self-awareness and competence and to reexamine the fit between you and your circumstances. Events for you may include active participation in community activities, becoming a grandparent, and taking up new interests and hobbies. In the late fifties and early sixties, some of your tasks are to accomplish your goals while there is still time and to adjust to the aging process. Some typical events are preparing for retirement and facing health problems. For most of you, your career will be waning in importance, but this is the time to work hard on relationships and worthwhile noncareer tasks, whether hobbies or church involvement.

Old age also brings its own tasks. These include preparing for the death of your spouse and indeed for your own death. Events include retirement, physical decline and a change in your finances.

God and Life Changes

Where does God and his purpose for our lives come into all of this? Without him, it all sounds a bit drear. And while these may be the phases of life common to humans, as Christians we have a different perspective on them.

As a young Christian adult, you will be setting life patterns, such as choosing a career and, perhaps, a spouse, which will affect the whole of your future walk with the Lord. This is the stage of life to establish yourself in a church as a responsible adult member of the congregation. In the next phase of life, it becomes important to consider the best place to live and work in order to help establish in the faith any children you may have.

If we look at the other end of our lives, for those taking early retirement, or even retirement at the normal age, there are new opportunities to serve the Lord during the remaining years of life. For many people these years often can be the most fruitful and fulfilling of all. With the increase in life expectancy, it is important to use these years well.

In missions we greatly benefit from, and appreciate, the service of countless folk in their fifties and sixties. Some go out to the mission field and help on work parties, building housing or administrative centers, for example. Others work in the mission headquarters—on maintenance or helping with domestic or secretarial work. All bring a lifetime of experience, and some have taken quite heavy administrative responsibilities.

The local church often has countless tasks and opportunities for service that older people can take up as well. Even in old age there is Hope spelled with a capital H. God always has meaningful tasks for us, and not in this life only! The New Testament picture of heaven is not one of sitting back on a cloud with a harp in your hand, but of worship and of service. In the parable of the talents the ones who have used their resources well were given extra responsibility: "Well done, good and faithful servant! You have been faithful with a few things; I will put you in charge of many things" (Mt 25:21).

Identifying Your Life Stage

In looking at your individuality, at what abilities God has given to you and at your natural gifts, you also need to bear in mind which stage you have reached in your life cycle. It may be that you are naturally gifted in caring for and listening to other people; you are a natural counselor. If you are in your twenties or thirties it may be most appropriate to use this in your professional life, as a nurse, a teacher or a social worker. If you are married and/or have children, the Lord has given you some ready-made "clients" for your caring skills. If, however, you are in your forties or fifties and have some free time and caring capacity, you may want to consider taking some counselor training. You may be able to use your abilities in the church or in the wider neighborhood.

Our work and the use of our gifts—natural and spiritual—must very much depend on where we are in our life cycle. We need to use our strengths and weaknesses appropriate to our age and stage. If you are young, enthusiastic and extraverted, it may be very appropriate to use evangelistic gifts in the secular world of your job, in an "open" youth group or in your neighborhood; or to use leadership gifts in the church youth fellowship. If you are retired and have extra time on your hands, it may be appropriate to use your administrative gifts in your local church office or organizational structure.

Our interests, as shown by the interest codes, have been proven to be pretty consistent throughout our life span. Nevertheless, there are appropriate and inappropriate ways to develop these at different stages in our lives. If you have strong Realistic interests, you may want to use these to help others who are less practical than you are. For example, some Realistic Christians, especially if they are young and energetic, help others with their car problems. However, if you are young, it is unlikely to be appropriate to use your Social interest as a counselor in the local church, although you can always be a good listener and a caring friend and become a counselor when you are more mature.

It is also true that what motivates us at one stage of our lives usually continues to motivate us at later stages, but there will be different ways of expressing our natural aptitudes. The things we are good at, that really motivate us, are in many ways transferable skills. We can transfer them from one occupation to another as we move through our life cycle, and from one hobby to another, or one act of service within the church to another.

Changing Values
Our value system—unlike our interests and natural aptitudes—may

change quite dramatically as we move through life. As we allow the Holy Spirit to work in us, he will be bringing our value system more into line with his. Many find that as their Christian commitment deepens, they wish that they didn't have to spend so much time and energy on their job so that they could serve the Lord full time instead. The Lord does call some into full-time service, but I believe he wants us to see our secular job as his service as well.

Does our personality change as we mature? To some extent, yes, but in many ways, no. God is at work in us, as much as we allow him to be, mellowing and refining our natural personality. Our temperament is derived from our genes plus the effect of our environment (life experiences). As we move through life our temperament will be modified. In addition, as was mentioned in the chapter on personality type, we can develop the less-developed side of our personality. However, I don't believe that God changes our personality for a different one, nor does he want us all to be clones. God is a creator who loves variety—look at the world around us. He did not intend a dog to behave like a cat!

Our individuality is not an excuse for sin. We don't have to give in to the natural weaknesses and temptations that beset our personality type. It is much better to get to know, understand and mature the unique personality that is ours.

Another important aspect of our lifelong journey is to set ourselves the goal of lifelong learning, regardless of our learning style. We see this pattern clearly in the Bible. God has never finished teaching us. The question is, Are we prepared to go on learning and growing? This also applies to "secular" learning. Let us not stagnate in middle age.

These days it is considered fairly normal to have two or three careers in our working lives. We need to think and plan for this, or plan to take early retirement and develop another side of ourselves, maybe in "full-time" Christian service.

Identifying Your Tasks

There are no tests in this chapter but there is an exercise, and a very important one. I want you to try to identify what tasks God has for you at this particular time. In order to think this through you will certainly need a place where you can be quiet and where you will not be disturbed. Your natural mind will enable you to determine some of these tasks, but you really need to listen to the Lord as well.

You need him to speak to you. It is easy to think that we know what tasks God has for us at a particular time, but when we are quiet before him we find that he has different perceptions from ours. Moses felt that he was called to rescue God's people. He set about it by killing the Egyptian. Moses had got his timing wrong, and he went about it in his own way instead of waiting for the Lord's way. God had a forty-year training program for him first.

In order to think about the tasks you face, start by listing the compartments of your life (work, home, family and so forth) and the roles you have. Here are two examples to show how it might work. Bear in mind that the two people featured in these examples are at particular stages in their life cycles. Their response to any situation will reflect their particular stage in life. Were they at different stages then their tasks and roles might be very different. You need to be thinking of what stage you are at in your own life cycle as you consider your life at this time.

The first example is a task list for a married man in his late thirties:

Work	Investigate a possible move either within or outside the company. (His work has been taking all his energy and time to the exclusion of his family and spiritual life.) Try for a job that has more regular hours.
Family	Spend more time with my wife and children. (God has been speaking to him about this recently. The children are now at an age when they need Dad around more.)

Spiritual life	Set aside a regular time to be with the Lord.
Personal life	Improve golf handicap. (He needs one good relaxing hobby.) Look into further training to upgrade job skills.
Church	See the minister and discuss my program. (He may need some fallow time from church commitments.)

Let's look at his life in relation to his roles—that is, what God has called him to *be* and not just to *do*.

Provider	I still have teenaged children and am the main wage earner. This is likely to be so for some time.
Husband	
Father	
Child of God	
Member of St. Peter's	

As he looks at the above perhaps God has laid on his heart one above all the others—maybe husband. He knows that he is not being what he could and should be to his wife. He is going to make this a particular matter of prayer. He is going to keep this aspect of what God has called him to be at the forefront of his mind. It will be the touchstone of his life in the coming year.

The second example is a task list for a single woman in her twenties:

Work	Need to consider further training. (Her schooling was disrupted and, anyway, was very different from her pre-ferred learning style. Her qualifications do not match her ability.)
Family	Feel that family relationships have been neglected and

	I need to spend more time with my brother and sister and their families.
Spiritual life	Get more involved in my local church.
Personal life	Get out and about more and make more friends.

Looking at her life in relation to her roles:

Employee
Daughter
Sister
Friend
Child of God
Member of the
   Community
   Church

As she looks at the above she realizes that she has been drifting through life without any clear-cut goals. She has allowed her introversion to cause her to withdraw from people in the family, in the church and in her personal life. To implement the above will take a considerable amount of energy and effort.

You should have a list of tasks that you believe God has called you to do at this time. In addition you should have an idea of the roles God has called you to fill. Maybe one of the roles or tasks should be particularly in focus at this time. Keep these details on a sheet of paper in your file so that you can use this information when you compile your personal profile.

Talking Points

1. Ask older members of the group to relate their experiences and how their tasks and roles have changed over the years. Others could then say

what their present roles are and how they are preparing to meet their future roles.

2. Is change inevitable for all of us? How can we prepare for and cope with changes in our lives? Discuss the changes Jesus had to undergo during his time on earth.

9

Warnings:
Are You
O.K.?

• • •

S ome years ago a popular book was published called *I'm OK—
You're OK.*[1] This book suggested four possible attitudes that we
can take up in relation to others.

I'm O.K.—You're not O.K.

I'm not O.K.—You're O.K.

I'm not O.K.—You're not O.K.

I'm O.K.—You're O.K.

While we may not agree with all the thinking behind this book, it is not
difficult to see these four positions in our own or others' behavior. We
hope that we can learn during childhood and adolescence to leave much
of the first three attitudes behind us, but probably each of us, to a
different degree, carries some of these attitudes over into our adulthood.
Our fears and insecurities cause us to adopt one of the above stances at
times. We hope the exercises in this book will have helped you to recognize your own worth, that you have gifts and talents given to you by

God. That is, that you can say, "I'm O.K."

One person will value some gifts more highly than another person does. Different cultures also vary in their evaluation of personality. For example, introversion is less valued in the United States and extraversion is less valued in Britain. As we have seen, churches have different corporate identities. Some, for example, lay major emphasis on an intellectual understanding of the gospel. Others focus on the emotions and lay emphasis on experiencing God. This may partly explain why we feel more at home in one denomination or church than in another. The secular world of today values certain attributes more than others. We have already discussed how physical strength and courage were valued in the days before modern technology. Today academic skills are very highly valued.

You may have heard the statement "He's only a . . . ," referring to someone's job. There is no biblical basis for downgrading anyone's talents. That we do not all have the same amount of talent is obvious from the parable of the talents (Mt 25). That we will not all be as attractive as each other is shown by the discussion of the parts of the body (1 Cor 12). Nevertheless, God values each person equally. We should value ourselves because of what God has made us and given to us, and believe that we can get joy and satisfaction by functioning in the way he has ordained for us.

Esteeming Ourselves and Others

The "I'm not O.K." syndrome results from a low self-image. Working through this book alone is unlikely to resolve this. It should help you to discover some of your gifts and talents. If your self-esteem is very low you may need to seek other help. The self-esteem measure in appendix eight may help you to determine your self-esteem level.

You may, alternatively, suffer from the "You're not O.K." syndrome, or both together ("I'm not O.K.—You're not O.K."). Whether our inner unresolved conflicts result in our blaming ourselves ("I'm not O.K.") or others ("You're not O.K.") depends in part on our personality traits. More passive personalities tend to blame themselves and more assertive personalities tend to blame others. Appendix eight also has a short measure to help you see if you have a predisposition to blame others for the things that threaten you in life.

Since we live in a fallen and damaged world and since none of us is completely whole, this book would be incomplete if we addressed the issue of talents but ignored the problem of the "damaged" personality. It is not my purpose to write extensively about damaged personalities. We do, however, want everyone who has worked through the exercises and produced a personal profile to realize that their emotional attitudes and their spiritual attitudes are also factors that will determine the degree to which they can reach the potential that God has for them.

Much has been written on inner healing and our psychological well-being, and it's good that God's people recognize their need of this. Christians have, in the past, been guilty of assuming that salvation means instant solutions to personal difficulties. This can lead to a denial of the fact that we still have facets of our lives that need "salvation," or healing, sometimes many years after we first became Christians.

We can think of one person who has all the gifts he needs to function happily, who makes a good contribution in his company and is appreciated by others. However, he sees himself as the "lowest of the low" and is continually saying—by his actions if not always in words—"No one appreciates me." Both his self-image and his view of other people are very damaged, and this is seriously affecting his personal relationships. Eventually others will believe his continuous message of "I'm not important" or "I'm no good." No amount of career help, no amount of affirmation by others is going to solve this problem. He needs help with the real problem, which is his own self-image.

People who feel that "others are not O.K." will also have difficulty using their full potential, as their personal relationships will be inadequate. Often they have the gifts and abilities to do a job but are passed over because they are unable to work well with others. This is doubly unfortunate because it reinforces the view that no one recognizes the person's gifts and that people do not appreciate him or her.

Before assuming that the difficulties you face are because people haven't understood your personality or who you are, consider whether these emotional factors are relevant to you. I think that understanding your personality and gifts will help you to grow and to reach your full potential.

Fulfillment

We do not have a right to total personal fulfillment. Maybe if we had lived in the Garden of Eden we would have experienced that. In looking at what "ought to be" or at God's original purpose, we need to be careful that we don't focus exclusively on this ideal. God has allowed us to live in a fallen, broken world, and we will experience pain, frustration and disappointment.

Pastor Richard Wurmbrand, who was imprisoned for many years, may not have felt that all his gifts were being given expression. When people give up well-paid jobs and fulfilling careers and go overseas to do mission work, they face many frustrations and privations and may not always find their potential realized.

Maybe circumstances dictate that you have a rather mundane, routine job, and you long to be and do something else. Only you can determine where God has called you and what he has called you to do. But we need to be prepared for the fact that God's call may not always lead to what we see as fulfillment. I believe it is right to seek to maximize those gifts God has given to us until we feel he has said, "No, this is where I want you now. I have things for you to do and to learn which can only be done in this situation." God is sovereign. We can rarely say with assurance, "This is his will for ever." Sometimes he allows frustration, even despair, in our lives, to reveal himself to us and in us.

Paul had great teaching and leadership gifts, and yet God allowed him to be imprisoned and eventually executed. Paul initially sought freedom, to further exercise his ministry. Then he accepted that God had purposes in his imprisonment, and many generations of Christians have benefited as a result. Without Paul's imprisonment we would have been without many of his letters and much of his teaching.

The need for fulfilling work, for affirmation, even for recognition, is basic to us. However, we cannot have these all the time and in all circumstances—to expect that is unrealistic. We can also have a need for purposeful activity, or for status or recognition, which is quite *in*appropriate. Some people, with major insecurity problems, are constantly seeking reassurance (by doing what others approve of) to bring them the affirmation they crave.

So in this case, as in all others, balance is needed. Yes, we can seek to use our gifts and talents; but there will be times of frustration when fulfillment is not possible—and God can bless these times to us also.

Workaholism

A warning should be sounded to those who have a tendency to *workaholism*. We have said that the need for meaningful work is a God-given need; it gives us purpose and significance. Does that mean if I work twelve hours a day, six days a week, I am fulfilling God's purpose and my own destiny even more? No, it's just as possible to abuse this need to work or to use it inappropriately, as any other need.

Our bodies need food, but we can use that need inappropriately in gluttony. Sexual expression is good and wholesome within the framework of God's purposes for it in marriage. We all know that this need can be, and is, abused. Similarly, work can be abused. Work is only one of the tasks that God gives us to do. He calls us to be members of families, members of the local church, members of our local community. To bury ourselves in our work to the exclusion of other activities is wrong, and usually points to some need in ourselves that we are seeking to meet in an inappropriate way.

False Modesty

It's hard to write in a Christian book that being very modest can be unhelpful. Some of us are naturally self-effacing and have retiring personalities; others are more bold and project ourselves and our attributes. When doing career counseling my job is harder with very modest people. I am trying to help them find out what they are good at while they have a value system that says you should never admit to being good at anything!

I have already stated that everyone needs affirmation. We need to know we are of value, and generally most of us profit from others affirming that we are valuable, not just for what we do, but for who we are. Self-esteem is a form of personal affirmation. What this means is that self-esteem is about being truthful about ourselves, acknowledging our strengths (the things we are good at) as well as admitting our weaknesses (the things we are not good at).

We know that God values us and we want others to value us, therefore we should value ourselves. A realistic self-esteem that is neither self-effacing nor boastful is healthy. We probably need good honest friends to help us in this. When you have completed your personal profile, go through it with a friend you can trust to be honest with you. Get his or her reaction to your self-evaluation. Listen to what he or she says without defending yourself. Some comments may suggest that you have more skills than you give yourself credit for. Other comments may suggest that you overestimate your abilities in some areas. We all need the feedback from others to get a good balance in this.

It is important that we do not bury our talent. This is spoken about in the parable of the talents (money), and we know that God is not pleased if we bury our talents (abilities). If we see children not developing to their full potential, we are concerned. God is similarly concerned when his children do not develop their potential. We hold back from using our talents for a variety of reasons, although perhaps fear of failure is the most common. If we don't risk, launch out, try for something, then we can't fail; this is a common defense mechanism.

Strengths As Weaknesses

We can use our personality traits, or strengths, inappropriately as well as in helpful ways. For example, you may have natural leading and directing skills, the ability to supervise others and achieve through them. Obviously this skill is necessary and good when used well, but it is possible to use it to control others and even to manipulate them, to use it when it's not required and when it would be more appropriate to sit back and let others do it, or even to be directed by others.

Similarly, your caring trait can lead to overprotectiveness of others, or even interference in others' lives. It can be used more for your own benefit, giving you the warm feeling of being needed.

For those of you who are of an independent nature, this independence can be a strength, but it can lead to self-sufficiency—an unwillingness to work with others in a team, submitting one to another.

In looking at the strengths God has given us and how we can use them to his glory, let us make sure we don't use them inappropriately to compensate for some inner need that's not being met elsewhere.

Weaknesses As Strengths

Conversely, our weaknesses also can be our strengths. Our reliance on the Lord grows when we have to operate in areas where we are not naturally comfortable. My major premise is that God normally wants us to use the natural gifts he has given us. However, he does sometimes put us in situations that seem far beyond our natural abilities.

Sometimes this is because we have dormant, undiscovered skills that we don't know we have, and God wants to dig these out and make us use and develop them. It's only in using gifts, often taking risks as we do so, that we can grow and develop and realize the full potential of our gifts.

At other times God wants to develop the "weaker" side of our personality so that we become more rounded. Many people with real leadership potential are strong people who can take a lot of pressure. Initially, however, they may not have all the sensibility to others that they need. Their own strength is in fact also a weakness. It's difficult to empathize with those who struggle with things that are no problem to you. I have seen these strong people grow and develop in this understanding and empathy, both through life's experiences or through taking training to develop their people-handling skills.

Many jobs need a broader range of skills than we naturally possess. This is particularly true on the mission field, where there is always more work to do than people to do it. When missionaries have to return home for sickness, furlough or whatever, the tasks have to be done by those who remain there, come what may. God gives us strength and anoints us with skills we don't naturally possess. Nevertheless, I believe that his normal purpose for us is to use our strengths as part of a body. However, he is sovereign and occasionally does seem to put us in situations where we appear to have no natural abilities.

Facing Failure
We will fail. It's important to accept failure, learn from it and get up and go on. The Bible is full of examples of people who failed and went on to do great things with God. Failure is a learning experience and can change us and mold us in ways that success never can, and in ways that all the courses in the world cannot do.

The learning cycle (chapter seven) began at feeling/sensing or experiencing. Who said that these had to be *positive* experiences? God, who allows us to experience things "so that we might know," allows us both good and bad experiences. Both are part of his plan for our growth and well-being.

When I think of failure in the Bible, David immediately springs to mind. He is mentioned as "a man after God's own heart," yet what he did to Uriah was very wrong, and he experienced the feeling of total failure (Ps 51). Jacob the deceiver, Peter's denial, Elijah under the juniper tree, Moses trying to free the Israelites in his own strength, Jonah trying to dodge God's call also come to mind, along with many others. Yet many of these are listed among those in Hebrews 11 who were still "living by faith" when they died.

Perhaps one of the clearest examples of failure as a learning experience is that of John Mark, whom Paul refused to take on his second missionary journey because he "had deserted them in Pamphylia and had not continued with them in the work" (Acts 15:38). John Mark must have "got up and gone on" and learned from this experience because we later read that Paul asked for Mark to be brought to him "because he is helpful to me in my ministry" (2 Tim 4:11).

Even the secular world acknowledges the importance of accepting failure. John Cleese, of Monty Python fame, who has moved into management training, writes, "In the healthiest organizations the taboo is not on making mistakes, it's on concealing them."[2] He even goes on to say that, far from being bad for you, mistakes can be good for you. "Any ego-loss suffered is more than compensated for by the ego-gain in showing you're the kind of guy who's big enough to admit when he's wrong." In the healthiest people, in the healthiest church, in the healthiest Christian organization there will be acceptance of failure.

Types of Failure

There seem to be two types of failure.

Real failure is where sin is involved. No one would doubt that David's adultery with Bathsheba was real failure. He had clearly broken God's law and therefore had truly failed himself and God.

Imaginary failure is where we have fallen below our own or others' expectations in terms of activity, output or behavior. If you only come third in an exam where you hoped to come first, this is surely imaginary failure.

With real failure we can ask for forgiveness from God and from other people involved and get up and go on. With imaginary failure we often have to question whether the expectations were right. Are they the Lord's? Is it just my pride that is hurt?

Failure can, of course, have elements of both real and imaginary failure in it. You forget to collect the children from school and when you get there they are unhappy and feel you have let them down. You need to say that you are sorry you forgot and to ask them to forgive you and to apologize to the teacher as well. However, it does not mean that you are a terrible parent and do not love your children—that would be having unreal expectations of yourself. If you hold on to these unreal expectations you will feel you have failed again and again.

I recently read through the Gospels looking for the signs of Jesus' humanity, especially the feelings and emotions he experienced in obeying the Father, being misunderstood by family, having opposition from political and religious sources, and so forth. I found that Jesus went through the whole range of experiences that we do, particularly as we respond to God's demands on our lives. Jesus could have suffered from a feeling of failure (imaginary failure: we know he knew no sin). How did he feel when Judas betrayed him, when Peter let him down, when his mother chided him? In all these cases there was always the potential for him to have felt he had failed, but he was always able to see the overview, the Father's purpose, and not just an egocentric view.

Jesus could have seen Judas's betrayal as a personal failure. Had he chosen the wrong person? What had he done wrong? Should he have spent more time explaining the nature of his task? Even Jesus may have been tempted in this way, but we know he overcame. Part of the over-coming process is to distinguish the real from the imaginary.

Strength and Weakness in the Scriptures

God has a lot to say about weakness in his Word. Most of it is opposite to what our Western culture says. God never appears to condemn us for being weak, nor to say that weakness is a sin. "He will take pity on the weak and the needy" (Ps 72:13). "He gives strength to the weary and increases the power of the weak" (Is 40:29). "Let the weakling say, 'I am strong!' " (Joel 3:10). "My grace is sufficient for you, for my power is made perfect in weakness" (2 Cor 12:9).

"The spirit is willing, but the body is weak" (Mt 26:41). (Jesus was disappointed that the disciples couldn't stay awake, but he didn't con-demn them.) "Those parts of the body that seem to be weaker are indis-pensable" (1 Cor 12:22). "For some say, 'His letters are weighty and forceful, but in person he is unimpressive [weak] and his speaking amounts to nothing' " (2 Cor 10:10). "If I must boast, I will boast of the things that show my weakness" (2 Cor 11:30). Those "whose weakness was turned to strength" (by faith) are listed in Hebrews 11.

There are at least twenty-three "Be strong" commands in the Word of God. Most of these are based on *God's* presence and strength. "Be strong in the Lord and in his mighty power" (Eph 6:10). "Be strong in the grace that is in Christ Jesus" (2 Tim 2:1).

Know your strengths and abilities. Don't depend on them; depend on God alone, but expect him to use and develop his creation in you. Accept your weakness. When circumstances put you in uncomfortable situations, trust God to give you the gifts you need. Accepting failure can be a growing experience.

Spiritual Attitudes

There are even more books written on spiritual growth than on emotional growth. For this reason I have not attempted to cover spiritual growth in this book. Nevertheless, it must be pointed out that, with all the career counseling help and all the emotional growth and wholeness we can achieve, it is ultimately our relationship and commitment to God through our Savior, Jesus Christ, that determines our reaching our full potential.

There seem to be two dangers into which we can fall. One is to over-spiritualize and see ourselves as worthless, with God doing everything in us and through us as though we were mere robots. The other is to overemphasize the natural, human-centered aspects and neglect the fact that without him we can do nothing (Jn 15:5).

It is my hope that you will take what you have learned about yourself through this book and *pray* about God's purpose for you, committing all that he has created in you back to him and asking him to work out his purposes in you and through you.

Talking Points

1. Discuss the concept of self-esteem and other-esteem. Is it possible to reach a point where we have a right esteem for both ourselves and others? How does God esteem us? Discuss the behavior characteristics of each of the four possible esteem positions:

I'm O.K.—You're not O.K.

I'm not O.K.—You're O.K.

I'm not O.K.—You're not O.K.

I'm O.K.—You're O.K.

2. Discuss workaholism—what it is and what effect it can have in our lives. Is it right to "burn ourselves out for God"?

3. Is failure inevitable? How can we handle it? Discuss cases of failure among Bible characters and how they coped with it. Is failure accepted in your group or church? What is God's attitude toward us when we fail him? Do we allow others to fail us and do we forgive them?

10

Putting It to Work

• • •

*O*ur focus so far has been mainly in two areas—our activities (what we *do*) and our aptitudes, values, interests and so forth (what we *are*). We have sought to try to match the two where possible. A further grid through which we can examine our activities is that of time.

To check whether you spend your time on activities that give you satisfaction, draw a pie chart similar to the one below. The titles given to the segments are guidelines, and you should choose your own titles to suit your activities. In the time circle, the size of the pie slice should be in proportion to the amount of time you spend on that activity.

Time Circle

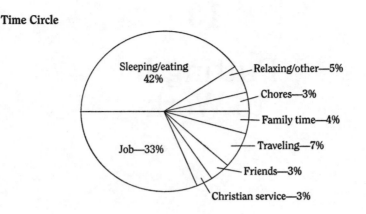

Now, in the same way, do a satisfaction pie chart, similar to the one below, again making the slices of the pie proportional to the degree of satisfaction each activity gives you.

Satisfaction Circle

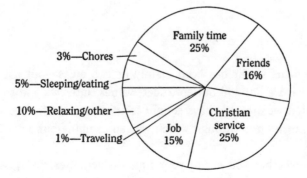

The person represented by the charts here gets a lot of satisfaction from family, friends and Christian service. Sleeping and eating are obviously not very satisfying. Work and traveling (to work) take up the vast majority of the time (excluding sleeping and eating) and leave very little time for the things that are satisfying (in this case, work is not a prime source of satisfaction).

This person may want to consider ways to change jobs to one that does not require traveling two hours each day. The present job also involves bringing work home and perhaps a new job wouldn't require this. This will leave a greater proportion of time for family, friends and Christian service.

In this case the saving on travel and job time is so great that there will be time for a special area of study (such as a Bible correspondence course). Economic needs allow for a slight drop in salary to achieve this. (See the Modified Time Circle chart.)

Modified Time Circle

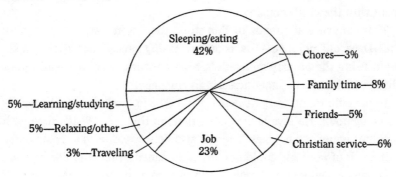

Now compare the time and satisfaction circles that represent your life—is there any large discrepancy? If there is, can it be altered? For example, you may spend fifty hours a week on a study program, but not really like it. However, you may consider this necessary to be qualified for a satisfying career. We do have to do things we do not like. Satisfaction is not an entitlement. Service and duty are a part of our calling too. Of course the practicalities of life mean that we often have responsibilities that give us little satisfaction, but which we have to do.

However, you do have some choice, and the purpose of looking at these charts is to consider if there is *appropriate* change that you can and should make. God's usual purpose for us is satisfaction in the tasks that he has set before us.

Dave was featured in *21st Century Christian*.[1] At twenty-nine he became one of the youngest bank managers in the country. A real high flier! As time went on the bank took more and more of his time—"bank first, family and personal life second" seemed to be the ethos of the bank and of his colleagues.

At the age of forty Dave decided to leave the bank, and a short while later he became a milkman. He has since been promoted to supervisor with responsibility for five rounds, but has resisted going into management with the milk company.

There are several strands to this story: there were values at the bank that Dave did not like—the company taking precedence over people, profit being the primary motivation, high pressure, deadlines—all values about which Dave became increasingly unhappy.

In his milk round work he gets up at 4:30 a.m. each day and is usually home by noon. He says he has more time on this job. "That's time with God, my family and hobbies. There is also no worry. I used to come home with loads of work and could not forget the targets, problems and hassle."

Dave changed jobs and took a drop in income in order to give himself more time to spend on things that were of value to him and that give him satisfaction. His satisfaction at the bank decreased as the pressures increased, and the values of the bank got more and more out of harmony with his own value system until the extra financial rewards were no compensation for these losses.

You may not be considering such a drastic change, but you do need to look at your life occasionally and see if God wants you to change direction. You may examine your life regularly, but if not, you may find the pie charts a help in focusing your thinking and in discerning God's purposes for you.

Who Am I?

One of the purposes of this book is to help you understand yourself better. This should help you to interact with the world around you more effectively. To understand yourself better is to appreciate all that God has done in you and for you.

If you gave a child a home computer as a birthday present and all he used it for was to play games on, you might feel he hasn't maximized the potential of your gift. That's what we are about here, maximizing God's gifts to us.

With tongue in cheek we can describe this as *anthropomaximology*—making the most of people. God has been in the business a long time. He wants to "make the most" of each one of us, not just because effective Christians glorify his name and extend his kingdom, but because he loves us. Like any creator, he gets pleasure when his creation fulfills its purpose and potential.

Your Personal Profile

As you have worked through each of the preceding chapters, you should have compiled a folder containing a summary of what your interests, natural aptitudes, values, personality type and learning style are, and a description of where you are in your life's journey. The sample profile in appendix nine should help you to summarize your data and produce your own personal profile.

This profile is a record of the work you have done and will help you to allow the information to become part of you so that you instinctively know yourself. For example, if the five natural gifts you found you have are

Buy/Sell

Negotiate/Liaise
Perform/Speak publicly
Develop/Build
Improve/Make better

then you may need to check these occasionally to ensure that you are using them well. The personal profile should also help you to ensure that you follow up and act on any possibilities that have arisen. It's easy to be enthusiastic but take no action, and in a year's time be no further forward.

It is important that you do not bury your profile among all your other papers, but make sure that you review it at regular intervals. You will not get the full benefit from the work you have done unless you do so. You may want to set yourself some goals to work on—and fix a date when you will evaluate progress made toward them!

God, Me, Others

If you have a correct view of yourself and a correct view of God, you also need a correct view of others. In other words, to function correctly you need to be able to say, mentally, to others, "You're O.K."

The work you have done, as recorded in your personal profile, can help you accept that others are both valuable and different. The Bible teaches that we have different gifts and the concept of personality types merely confirms this.

We all pay lip service to the concept of our individual differences. But while we accept our own individuality and uniqueness, we still have difficulty accepting that others are different. We slip into the attitude that if everyone was like me, it would be fine. Of course we know that this isn't true, but our attitudes and behavior often tell another story!

Most of us need help in seeing how we can serve others and how others can serve us. That is, to recognize our *interdependence.* Sometimes as Christians we are too *independent,* doing our own thing. Sometimes we are too *dependent,* expecting others to meet our spiritual and emotional needs and even, in certain types of church, to make our decisions for us. God has called us, however, to live in *interdependence* with others and to be *dependent* on him.

Consider the parameters we looked at in chapter six:

Introverts need extraverts	Extraverts need introverts
Sensors need intuitives	Intuitives need sensors
Thinkers need feelers	Feelers need thinkers
Perceivers need judgers	Judgers need perceivers

Consider the interest codes (chapter three). We need the practical (Realistic) person to look after the plant and fixtures, the Investigative person to think things through, envisage possible futures and have ideas. We need the Artistic to create, the Social to care (even though we all have this responsibility, some are more naturally gifted), the Enterprising to organize and manage, and the Conventional to keep the system going and loyally serve the group.

As we see from the personality and other measures we have looked at, no one has all the gifts. We all score very differently. *Together* we can make it. Individually we are incomplete.

God has created us for *corporate* living (1 Cor 12:27). This does not necessarily mean that we all share one house or one purse, but that our lives should form part of a living organism, the body of Christ. Your job, your family life, your social and recreational life, your church life are all parts of a living organism.

God's Groups for You

When you, as an individual, function correctly, the groups that God has called you to be a part of function better. As these groups function better the entities that they are a part of will function better also. Our families are cells that help give cohesion to the local community. If your family is not functioning well, you can be a part of helping to bring reconciliation and understanding to it—healing between each member and God and one member and another. That well-being will spill over into the community.

Similarly, in our social and recreational life the groups that we belong to will function better when we know ourselves and function well. In our church life, when our gifts complement those of others and when we work with others, acknowledging their gifts, the whole body will function better, bringing greater glory to our God and Father.

Through your job you are contributing to the national economy that keeps us all fed, clothed and protected. You are a witness for God in the world. However, your work is more than just an opportunity to witness. It is one of the places where you can express and use the gifts that God has given to you. It is where you can contribute to God's world.

As each member of the body grows and reaches fuller potential, the total body is healthier, be it family, church, community or nation. Personal growth can seem like a selfish exercise, but as we each function as we are designed to, we shall be of greater service and help to those around us.

Maximizing Your Potential in the Local Church

Great strides have been made in Britain in recent years in moving from "one-person ministry" to involving all the congregation in the ministry of the local church. Many of us can look back to the time when "lay" jobs consisted of keeping the graveyard tidy, maintaining the fabric of the church, looking after business and finance matters, and the like. All of the "spiritual" jobs were done by the minister. The local church minister could sometimes be seen as "the bottleneck" rather than as the leader who stimulated others into activity.

Think of a church of around two hundred adults and assume that each one gives ten hours of his or her time each week in being part of the church. This means a labor force equivalent to fifty full-time people. Quite a management exercise! Fortunately greater lay involvement has meant the expertise of those with management experience is now being employed to help use people's skills more effectively. Administry, details of which can be found in appendix two, has been a help to many churches in this respect. It sounds rather clinical to talk of making better use of people. Releasing our potential to serve, and to get joy and satisfaction in serving, is far nearer the truth.

Do We Value the Gifts Equally?

In both church and mission we need to look again at the value we place on certain jobs. It's difficult to get people to do the jobs that are seen as lowly and less glamorous. Who is going to put the hymn books out, make the tea and coffee, paint and maintain the buildings in the local church? Who wants to be a typist, or look after the office records in the mission? We all need affirmation. The Bible teaches quite clearly that the body of Christ needs all the parts, not just the glamorous ones, to function in order to be healthy and whole (1 Cor 12).

There seem to be two answers. One is to divide the work into *service* and *ministry*. The service jobs are like household chores, those that have to be done on behalf of all the members to enable the church to function. Ministry jobs are those that have a more overtly spiritual function or greater prominence. Perhaps each church member should have a balance of service and ministry jobs.

The second approach is to believe wholeheartedly in the principle that all jobs are of equal value to God and the Christian community. The preacher is a part of the body as is the treasurer. Those who run the social functions are as valuable as those who organize and oversee the house groups.

Unless we increase the motivation of those in the more mundane and backroom work, the "workforce" will continue to desire to seek to do only the high profile jobs. Most local church leaders will confirm that people want to counsel, teach or lead, but it's difficult to get anyone to do the "bread and butter" jobs.

In my own mission, our centers are run by hard-working folk who put in long hours providing basic services (housing, lifts to airports, renewing visas, buying and shipping, typing and office services, and so on). The Bible translators get much more emotional payoff in terms of affirmation and even, often, in financial support. I must add that they have a very tough job and do usually appreciate the work of the support team that keeps them in their village assignment and work. But the people in the "support" roles themselves need to be supported and affirmed.

Somehow we need to get back to the biblical principle that we are a team, a body, and all parts are to be valued equally. We need more thanks, more words of appreciation, more affirmation for those who work in the less-recognized areas. We do appreciate them. We do need them. Let's say so and act as if we believed it.

Each one of God's children is a precious and unique creation. People say, "I don't have any gifts." "I can't do very much." Nonsense! God doesn't make that sort of person. Let's see people discover their unique gifts and talents and value themselves for who they are. Let the Christian community value the gifts of all and try to eradicate the hierarchical view of gifts.

First Peter 4:10 says: "Each one should use whatever gift he has received to serve others, faithfully administering God's grace in its various forms." Let's help each other to discover our gifts, not by the world's values but by God's standards. And remember, God values gifts equally. He can use them all when they are dedicated to his service.

In the parable of the talents, all are encouraged to use their gifts faithfully. The man with only one talent seems to need help to accept that although his gift from God seems, to some, to be small, he should use it faithfully.

Commitment of Time and Talents

My local church has an annual gift and commitment Sunday when we consider what we will give to God's work. A list is given to the members which reads as follows:

I would like to give (or continue to give) in the following areas:

1. In the area of worship; singing, playing musical instruments, reading, dance, drama, prayers

2. In the area of youth work; nursery, Sunday school, Pathfinders

3. In the area of caring; visiting, babysitting, transportation, helping with meals

4. In the area of serving; sidesman, bookstall, library, tapes, audiovisual

5. In the area of helping; coffee, washing up, cleaning, typing, collating, maintenance, gardening

6. Further areas

If you would like to know more about any of the above please indicate here—

You may care to do something similar in your church, if it's not already done. You can probably add other areas of service to the list above.

Other churches I know have one person (or even a small committee) appointed to look after all job allocations in the church. We go to great effort when making a paid appointment in the church (youth worker, lay worker, curate, and so forth). A job description is drawn up and various people are interviewed to try to find someone with the right talents and experience for it.

If the local church is using the equivalent of fifty full-time people's time, given by the congregation, should we not also invest some time and energy in seeing that those people are encouraged in using their skills well?

I would like to see our churches get to the point where every committed church member has an annual review with the minister or senior elder.

This review would include what the member is doing in the church, what he or she feels about this activity and which areas of ministry he or she would like to move into in the future. Sometimes the local church is understaffed because the motivation to use our natural gifts in the Lord's work has not been tapped.

Lack of Motivation

If we look at a list of why people do not give time and energy to the local church, it could include:

1. Lack of commitment to Jesus
2. Hurts, frustrations and discouragements in the church
3. Poor management—they are not clear on what's expected of them, who does what and so forth
4. Pastoral care needs not met—they are having a difficult time in life generally
5. The "I don't have anything to offer" syndrome

Numbers 2-5 could be addressed in a review time, and even number 1, if the interviewer has the right skills.

Yet we need to keep in mind problems of the "one man band" minister (is he or she pastor, teacher, organizer/administrator, and so on?). The concept of a team ministry, using all of the congregation's gifts, is a key to having a healthy church.

The career measures in this book have been successfully applied in teaming. We have used career guidance profiles as a starting point for discussion with Christians who want to work together closely as a team, to complement each other's gifts. Recognizing what God has given to each one on the team, and not competing with one another, can lead us to appreciate and to enjoy each other's contribution.

If no one in the team has a particular skill that is needed, then perhaps by prayer and discussion one person can be encouraged to develop latent skills or acquire learned skills to meet this need. While this person is growing in these skills the others should be encouraging and understanding that she is working in skill areas where she is not yet totally comfortable.

We need each other. Let's ask the Lord to increase our appreciation of one another. Let's ask him to enable each one of us to encourage and help others to grow, as well as maximize our potential for him.

Where Do You Go from Here?

God's concern and desire for each person is bound up with the answer to a question: "What is it that I can or should be doing?" The answer to that question can be presented as follows:

What it is that I can or should be doing?	=	1 knowing God	+	2 knowing myself	+	3 knowing my abilities	+	Plan of action to continually correct 1, 2 and 3

Knowing is more than intellectual knowledge. It is a deeper understanding than that. You need to be at peace with yourself, to know "I'm O.K." You need to know your uniqueness and gifts, those talents God has given to you. It's not wishing to be anyone else, but accepting gratefully what he has given you as a sacred trust to be used for him.

Above all, you need to know God. His purposes for you are good. "For I know the plans I have for you . . . plans to prosper you and not to harm you, plans to give you hope and a future" (Jer 29:11). So let's discover God's plans for us!

Set Aside a Day

It is easy to ask God to "bless us and make us what he wants us to be" and then sit back and wait for it to happen. Yet God has given us control over our own bodies and even our own personal growth and development. He does change us, often through difficulty or interaction with others, but there is a point where we decide or determine it will happen, a point where we become part of the answer to our prayers. Before you finish this book, you will find it helpful to write down some future goals.

You may want to take your personal profile, and any other ideas or suggestions you have gained from this book, and spend a quiet day before the Lord praying over the gifts God has given you and the tasks in life he has sent you. The profile is a large amount of data, and you may wish to highlight the parts of it that God has particularly laid on your heart at this time. Leviticus 16:29-30 reads, "This is a permanent law: You must do no work on the twenty-fifth day of September, but must spend the day in self-examination and humility . . . for this is the day commemorating the atonement, cleansing you in the Lord's eyes from all of your sins" (LB).

Our focus must be on the giver, not the gifts. The day referred to above was set aside by Jewish law to commemorate the atonement. This refers to the death of Jesus for you to "cleans[e] you in the Lord's eyes from all of your sins" (v. 30). "You are not your own; you were bought at a price" (1 Cor 6:19-20). The basis of our acceptance is the cross.

"This ceremony, in later generations, shall be performed by the anointed High Priest" (Lev 16:32 LB). Jesus is now our anointed High Priest. It is to him that we go with all that we have and all that we are and offer it back to him. Only as our lives are surrendered to him can our gifts be accepted and used in his service.

Build a Memorial

When Israel had learned something specific from God, he told them to build a memorial so that they would not forget what he had taught them. When the Lord had taken the Israelites over the Jordan, they were told to take twelve stones from the middle of the river and that "these stones are to be a memorial to the people of Israel forever" (Josh 4:7).

You have put a lot of effort in working through this book, and it would be a pity if that effort was wasted by not applying what you have learned in the years ahead. The Israelites were to remember every time they saw the pile of stones that God had parted the waters for them. It will help you to review regularly these materials, your goals and any actions you have decided upon. Your "pile of stones" could be a note in your diary each month, or a slip of paper in your Bible with some key words on it that remind you of the goals you have set for yourself.

May God richly bless you as you seek to maximize the wonderfully created being that you are.

Talking Points

1. Discuss time management and how various members of the group feel about their use of time. Some may be willing to draw a time circle of how their week is divided up among the various categories and compare this with how much satisfaction they get from each. Should we expect to get satisfaction from all of our activities? Is the Lord interested in our having a balanced lifestyle? (Who decides what is balanced?)

2. Discuss the concept of teamwork in the light of the Bible's teaching on our being a body. Using the personal profiles that each should have been able to produce after working through this book, discuss how you can supplement each other's gifts and abilities.

3. Discuss what use your church or group makes of the gifts of those who belong to it. Are you making the most of the potential the Lord has given you both as individuals and as a body? What can you do to use those gifts to greater effect?

4. Do you have difficulty finding people to do the "dirty" or "menial" jobs in your church? Discuss ways of overcoming this—perhaps more teaching on valuing all gifts equally and on our attitudes toward serving. Could everyone have a share of the ministry and the service jobs? How can you motivate members to each play a part rather than leaving most of the work to a few of the people?

Appendix 1

Career Counseling
and the Use of
Psychometric Tests

• • •

Types of Career Counseling

There are two main approaches to career counseling—differentialist and developmental. The former seeks to measure a person's aptitudes and skills and match them to a job. This tends to fit the layperson's view that there is a certain job somewhere that exactly fits his or her personality and skills, and that when he or she finds it all will be well. Diagramatically this can be viewed like this:

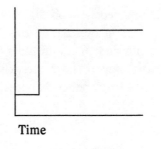

Time

The developmental approach, which I use, sees the whole of life as a series of growth steps in understanding oneself and applying and using that knowledge. This also can be represented diagrammatically.

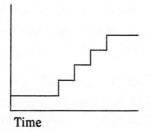

Time

This fits much better with what we know of how people develop through life: they have different goals and appropriate tasks at different stages of life. My own style of career counseling combines several approaches. Imagine that you had come to me for career counseling; together we would use and explore:

Psychometric tests and other measures—By using a variety of these and looking for a general pattern, we gather data that can be compared with your life experience. You would then have to validate this material as being a fair representation of yourself.

Examining your life experience—We would look at choices made at school, jobs enjoyed and disliked, places where you have succeeded and failed. Your life experience is a very valuable part of the process.

Personal counseling—In working with many people the career counselor gains experience, and this experience is an important part of the career counseling process.

The Use of Psychometric Tests

A psychometric test is, as the word suggests, a measure of human behavior. The word *test* immediately puts some people off. Can they fail? No, certainly not. There are no right or wrong answers, and it's often best to give your immediate "gut" reaction rather than think too long about the answer. The terms *exercises, measures* and even *inventories* are all used to avoid the suggestion that people are being tested.

For example, let us assume that you are trying to find out where you lie on the Introvert/Extravert scale. Do you prefer the inner world of ideas and concepts (Introverts) or the outer world of people and things (Extraverts)? Obviously we all work in both, but which is your preference, the one you use most and more easily? A well-researched set of questions about your behavior patterns can help you to establish which you prefer and indicate some measure of the strength of that preference in relation to other people's preferences.

Can We Trust the Result?

There are two mistakes you can make in relation to such tests. One is to believe them; the other is to disbelieve them! They are a tool that, if properly used, can serve us. No test is 100 percent accurate. No scale can adequately represent a unique, complex personality; but it can be a useful tool in beginning to understand it.

The interest test (chapter three and appendix three) has been used for a number of years and has been found to be reliable (in that approximately the same result is usually obtained when one person does the test on two or more occasions). Validity (does it measure what it says it measures?) is more difficult to check. But most people using the interest test are happy with the result when checking it against the RIASEC descriptions.

All the other tests in this book are to help you to consider concepts, not to produce a result. In every case you should look at the results and see if *you* think they are correct. If you feel that the results do not accurately reflect you, then you should question the accuracy of your results. The results should agree with your actual life experience.

Can They Be Faked?

Career counseling has been shown to be one of the most valid uses of psychometric tests. In other uses of tests, such as when a person is being interviewed for a job, one may wish to give a modified impression of himself or herself. The person being interviewed for a sales job may wish to score high on social skills. The person being interviewed for a management post may wish to score high on leadership skills.

However, in career counseling the only person you will fool by giving inaccurate answers is yourself! You are trying to get an accurate picture of yourself so that you can view yourself realistically and set good goals for your life. So it's in your interest to answer all the tests and measures as honestly as possible. You will get the best result by giving your quick "gut" reaction. Sometimes it helps to get your spouse (if you're married) or a good friend who knows you well to look them over afterwards and see if you have given realistic answers.

Self-Evaluation and Observation

Assume that we are trying to evaluate whether a person has a preference for shyness or boldness. We could ask him a whole series of questions as to how he reacts to certain situations and use the results to score him on the following scale.

Shy — — — — — — — —|— — — — — — — Bold
     0   1   2   3   4   5   6   7   8   9   10

In addition to such a test we could also ask the person simply to choose for himself the score that is most appropriate. Such self-evaluation (or observation) has been found to be as accurate as "testing" for people who are fairly well educated and self-aware. Where possible we have tried to use both methods in this book.

Let's say you scored 2 on the above scale in the test. When you read the description of "shy" and "bold" you feel that you *are* shy, but not to that degree, and you rate yourself 4. Your friends agree with your assessment so you leave the result at 4.

Why Use Tests?

Many well-researched tests have been used over decades and have produced much useful data both in terms of the concepts they represent and the people they are measuring. Tests are useful in producing comparative data on large groups. For example, use of the Myers Briggs Type Indicator has shown that a majority of Americans are extraverts and a majority of British are introverts. It would be impossible to produce this type of data by self-evaluation.

Another reason for using tests is that some people are not very self-aware and would not be able to describe themselves adequately in terms of the concepts being measured. The shy or bold scale would be easier for most of us to use than, for example, a measure of how we make decisions using thinking or feeling judgments.

Appendix 2

Resources

• • •

General

1. Richard Bolles. *What Color Is Your Parachute?* Rev. ed. Berkeley, Calif.: Ten Speed Press, 1991. A practical manual for job-hunters and career changers. Over two million copies sold in the U.S. Deals more with the mechanics of career change than with identifying skills.

2. Howard Figler. *The Complete Job-Search Handbook.* New York: Holt, Rinehart and Winston, 1979. Deals more with the skills needed to get a job than with identifying your own abilities.

3. Leslie Morphy. *Career Change.* Cambridge: Hobsons Publishing, 1987. A CRAC (Careers Research and Advisory Centre) publication. A British book covering such topics as current changes in employment patterns, women returning to work, alternatives to full-time employment and lots of practical data such as books, places, people, addresses and so forth.

4. Gary Friesen and Robin Maxson. *Decision Making and the Will of God.* Portland, Ore.: Multnomah Press, 1986. The traditional view of God is that he has one perfect will for our lives. This book presents an alternative. A

small study guide is published with it for use by individuals or groups.

5. Leland Ryken. *Work and Leisure in Christian Perspective*. Portland, Ore.: Multnomah Press, 1988. A thorough exploration of the issues of work and leisure from a Christian point of view.

Interests

1. John Holland. *Making Vocational Choices: A Theory of Careers*. Englewood Cliffs, N.J.: Prentice Hall, 1973. Sets out Holland's theory of interest themes and types with research evidence. Appendices include his Self-Directed Search test and an occupational classification according to Holland's themes.

2. Gary Gottfredson, John Holland and Deborah Kimiko Ogawa. *Dictionary of Holland Occupational Codes*. Palo Alto, Calif: Consulting Psychologists Press, 1982. A comprehensive listing of over 12,000 jobs and their RIASEC coding.

Natural Aptitudes

1. Ralph Mattson and Arthur Miller. *Finding a Job You Can Love*. New York: Thomas Nelson Publishers, 1982. The authors believe that our "motivated gifts" are the prime measure in determining our life's activities. The book seeks to help you find these and "put into perspective your own inclinations and God's will for you."

Values

1. Louis Raths, Merrill Harmin and Sidney Simon. *Values and Teaching*. Columbus, Ohio: Charles E. Merrill, 1966.

Personality Type

1. Isabel Briggs Myers and Peter B. Myers. *Gifts Differing*. Palo Alto, Calif.: Consulting Psychologists Press, 1980. Sets out the theory of personality type with particular reference to the Myers Briggs Type Indicator.

2. Harold Grant et al. *From Image to Likeness*. New York: Paulist Press, 1983. The authors are involved in Catholic mission and have used the MBTI in this context. There is a chapter on each of the four functions (sensing/intuition/feeling/thinking), with exercises to help us develop our weaker functions. The authors seek to link these functions with the characteristics of the Godhead.

3. David Keirsey and Marilyn Bates. *Please Understand Me*. Del Mar, Calif.: Prometheus Nemesis Book Company, 1984. An easy-to-read book explaining psychological type in relation to Carl Jung and to Myers Briggs. Applies theory to mating, children and leadership styles. Contains a self-administered temperament sorter yielding an MBTI type result.

4. Isabel B. Myers and Katharine Briggs. *Myers Briggs Type Indicator*. Palo Alto, Calif.: Consulting Psychologists Press. This indicator is only usually available to those trained in its use. Oxford Psychologists Press sells it in the U.K.

5. Chester Michael and Marie Norrisey. *Prayer and Temperament*. Charlottesville, Va.: Open Door, 1984. This book links different prayer forms to different temperament types.

Learning Styles

1. Gordon Lawrence. *People Types and Tiger Stripes*. Gainesville, Fla.: Center for Applications of Psychological Type, 1979. CAPT has been serving since 1975 as a center for research, education and services connected with the MBTI. This particular book applies type theory to learning styles and education.

2. Bernice McCarthy. *The 4 MAT System*. Barrington, Ill.: Excel, 1980. A good introduction to learning styles—tries to harmonize research from diverse fields. Applies both left/right brain and learning style research to teaching techniques.

3. Peter Honey and Alan Mumford. *The Manual of Learning Styles*. Maidenhead, Berks., U.K.: Ardingly House, 1984. This book is used by those

engaged in management training. It contains their Learning Style Questionnaire.

4. Pat Guild and Stephen Garger. *Marching to Different Drummers.* Alexandria, Va.: Association for Supervision and Curriculum Development, 1985. This book aims to help educators understand learning styles and implement this knowledge in their teaching and curriculum.

5. David A. Kolb. *Experiential Learning—Experience as the Source of Learning and Development.* Englewood Cliffs, N.J.: Prentice Hall, 1984. A comprehensive statement on learning theory that includes much research data.

6. Russell D. Robinson. *Helping Adults Learn and Change.* West Bend, Wis.: Omnibook, 1979. Brings into one book most current teaching on how adults learn. Practical and clearly presented.

7. Charles Claxton and Patricia Murrell. *Learning Styles.* College Station, Tex.: ASHE/Texas A&M University, 1987. A succinct book summarizing current learning style theories and applying these in higher education. The book takes good account of the fact that learning style theory is still in the developmental stage.

Appendix 3

Interest
Test

• • •

Section 1—Interest Type Characteristics

Rank yourself on the following interest type characteristics according
to the degree to which the statement is true of you: 1 = almost never,
2 = sometimes, 3 = almost always.

_____ 1. Prefer well-ordered environments.
_____ 2. Like to work with individuals and with groups.
_____ 3. Uncomfortable in social settings.
_____ 4. Strong drive to attain organizational or personal goals.
_____ 5. Value beauty and aesthetic qualities.
_____ 6. Have strong interpersonal skills.
_____ 7. Weak in leadership skills.
_____ 8. Confident of intellectual abilities.
_____ 9. Save money or buy conservative things (furniture, houses).
_____10. Responsive to feelings of others.

_____ 11. Like art, music, drama, other creative interests.

_____ 12. Prefer free, unstructured situations; averse to rules.

_____ 13. Mechanically and athletically inclined with good physical coordination.

_____ 14. Prefer practical to theoretical problems.

_____ 15. Enjoy academically challenging tasks.

_____ 16. Prefer to work independently.

_____ 17. Enjoy making things happen.

_____ 18. Value prestige and power.

_____ 19. Attend lots of workshops and other group experiences.

_____ 20. Weak verbal and interpersonal skills.

_____ 21. Like to be held accountable.

_____ 22. Like systematic verbal and numerical activities.

_____ 23. Avoid ambiguous and nonconforming situations.

_____ 24. Use artistic means for self-expression.

_____ 25. High respect for authority.

_____ 26. Have teaching ability and enjoy helping others to grow.

_____ 27. Enjoy ethical discussions and activities.

_____ 28. Concerned with welfare of others.

_____ 29. Tend to be reserved and introspective.

_____ 30. Tend to be both stable and practical.

_____ 31. Not interested in "personal growth" activities.

_____ 32. Good verbal, persuasive, entrepreneurial skills.

_____ 33. Value money, material possessions and status.

_____ 34. Averse to free, unsystematic, exploratory behavior in new areas.

_____ 35. Individualistic.

_____ 36. Dislike routine/procedural occupations.

_____ 37. Avoid work involving long periods of intellectual effort.

_____ 38. Concerned with leadership and responsibility.

_____ 39. Like to build things with tools.

_____ 40. Like to work outdoors.

_____ 41. Leave leadership to others.

_____ 42. Lack both scientific and mechanical ability.

_____ 43. Willing to take risks to try something new.

_____ 44. Most effective at well-defined tasks.

_____ 45. Enjoy treating and healing others.

_____ 46. Spend money and time on cars, motorcycles, boats

_____ 47. High energy level.

_____ 48. Scientific orientation.

_____ 49. Task-oriented, wrapped up in work.

_____ 50. Dislike science and systematic thinking.

_____ 51. Dress in freer styles than other people.

_____ 52. Not assertive about own capabilities.

_____ 53. Think through rather than act out problems.

_____ 54. Strong need to understand the world.

Indicate, beside each question number below, the number of points you awarded. Add the figures in each column to obtain the six totals.

Theme	R	I	A	S	E	C
	3	7	5	2	4	1
	13	8	11	6	17	9
	14	15	12	10	18	22
	20	16	24	19	21	23
Questions	30	29	35	26	32	25
	31	48	36	27	37	33
	39	49	43	28	38	34
	40	53	51	42	47	41
	46	54	52	45	50	44
Totals						

Record your totals in the space labeled "Score" below. Then write a number in the space labeled "Rank," giving six points to the theme on which you scored highest, five points to the second, etc. See the Note on the answer sheet below on how to rank themes having the same score.

Theme	R	I	A	S	E	C
Score						
Rank						

Now transfer the ranking to the answer sheet below.

Section 2—Actions Card Sort

This section uses our actions (what we do) to help determine our preferred interest type. At the end of this appendix are 54 action verbs that relate to our interests and also the numbers 1 to 6. You have three options for producing a set of "action" cards.

1. Cut them out from the book.
2. Photocopy them and cut them up.
3. Copy them by hand onto notecards or paper and cut them up.

If you make your own, make sure that the theme letters on the back appear exactly as they do in the book. When you have the cards, find a large surface, either a table or the floor. Place the "head cards" numbered 1 to 6 across the top, like this:

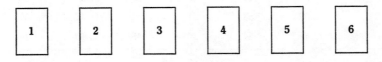

Now take the cards with the actions on them. You need to place each one under one of the numbers at the top, according to the degree to which this verb describes activities in which you are interested, and therefore you often do and enjoy doing. The more you enjoy a particular activity, the higher up you need to put that card, from number 1 for least interest/enjoyment to number 6 for most interest/enjoyment. Try not to let yourself be influenced by the theme letters on the backs of the cards.

For example, one card says "Repair." Maybe you repair clocks, cars, electrical equipment, socks, shirts or whatever. You like to engage in the practical activity of repairing. If this is a major interest activity for you place it under 5 or even 6. If this is of no interest or little interest, place it under 2 or even 1. If this action is of only moderate interest, then under 3 or 4.

When you have finished, make a small chart like the one shown as an example below, with the numbers 1 to 6 across the top and the theme letters, R I A S E C, down the side. Turn the cards over under number 1 and count how many cards of each of the six letters you placed under it—that is, how many R cards, I cards, A cards and so on. Record these on the chart as in the example below. Repeat for numbers 2 to 6.

Theme	1	2	3	4	5	6
R	-	-	-	-	4	5
I	-	-	-	2	4	3
A	5	3	1	-	-	-
S	2	5	2	-	-	-
E	-	1	2	6	-	-
C	-	3	4	2	-	-

Multiply these numbers by the value of the head card to get a subtotal. Add the subtotals in each of the six rows to determine the points awarded to each theme letter, as in the example chart below. This gives a total for each of the six themes.

Theme	1	2	3	4	5	6	Total	Rank
R	.	.	.	.	$4 \times 5 +$	5×6		
	.	.	.	.	$(20) +$	$(30) =$	50	6
I	.	.	.	$2 \times 4 +$	$4 \times 5 +$	3×6		
	.	.	.	$(8) +$	$(20) +$	$(18) =$	46	5
A	$5 \times 1 +$	$3 \times 2 +$	1×3	.	.	.		
	$(5) +$	$(6) +$	(3)	.	.	. $=$	14	1
S	$2 \times 1 +$	$5 \times 2 +$	2×3	.	.	.		
	$(2) +$	$(10) +$	(6)	.	.	. $=$	18	2
E	.	$1 \times 2 +$	$2 \times 3 +$	6×4	.	.		
	.	$(2) +$	$(6) +$	(24)	.	. $=$	32	4
C	.	$3 \times 2 +$	$4 \times 3 +$	2×4	.	.		
	.	$(6) +$	$(12) +$	(8)	.	. $=$	26	3

Add a rank for the six totals, giving 6 points to the type with the highest score, 5 to the second highest, etc., down to 1 point to the lowest. Transfer the results of this ranking to the answer sheet below.

Section 3—Birds of a Feather
We have a tendency to be drawn toward people who have similar interests to ourselves. Assume that you are at a conference where people are divided into six seminars. These seminars are discussing general topics and enjoying social interaction. The seminar groups are labeled R, I, A, S, E and C, as follows.

Group R—These are practical people. They are good with their hands—enjoying carpentry, mechanics, domestic crafts, machinery, tools. Some are athletic, and most like outdoor activities. Some personality characteristics are conformity, straightforwardness and dependability. They like to see tangible results to their work.

Group I—These are academic people. They investigate, analyze, evaluate and like to solve puzzles and problems. They live in the world of concepts and ideas. Some personality characteristics are independence, criticism, rationality. They have a need to know and to find the answer.

Group A—These people are highly imaginative with innovative abilities. They do not work well in highly structured environments and like to be "free spirits." Some of them are "arty," although architects and other creative people also feature here. Some personality characteristics are emotionalism, originality, nonconformity and impulsivity. They have a need to express themselves.

Group S—These people like to work with people, to train, care for and empathize with them. They are found in the nursing, teaching and caring professions. Some personality characteristics are patience, responsibility and friendliness. They like to be needed by others.

WARNING—Because the S theme has so many Christian virtues, it is easy for Christians to overidentify here. If this is not a natural inborn interest theme for you it does not mean that you are less Christian. Many people in the secular world score highly in this theme, but they have no Christian commitment.

Group E—These people like to work on people and through people. They make natural managers. They may range from business types to the full-blown entrepreneur. They can be persuasive, and coordinate and arrange events and activities well. Some personality characteristics are ambition, dynamism, optimism and self-confidence. They have a desire to influence others.

Group C—These people like to work with data. They have clerical and numerical ability. They are faithful, work hard, and put in long hours. They keep the organization running smoothly. Some personality characteristics are conscientiousness, orderliness, stability and conservatism.

They like and need structure, and help provide it.

Choose which of the six seminar groups it would be your first choice to attend and place a 6 on the appropriate column of the third row of the answer sheet below. This group has to leave the conference and you are asked to choose another group to attend. Indicate by placing a 5 under this group. Again this group has to leave (nothing personal, we hope!) and you are asked to choose from the four remaining groups. This continues until you have a list of your preferences for associating with these six different groups of people.

Interest Test Answer Sheet

Theme	R	I	A	S	E	C
Section 1 (by characteristics)						
Section 2 (by actions)						
Section 3 (by affinity)						
Total						

Note: If two themes have the same score, then average the score. So if R and I rank first award them 5 1/2 points each, since the first should get 6 points, the second 5, and the average of 6 and 5 is 5 1/2.

Add together the figures in the six columns (that is, add the ranking figure from each of the three tests) to get a total. Which three themes have the largest totals? Your interest code is the three letters ordered as largest, second largest, third largest. Write it in the boxes below:

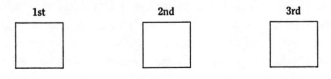

Now turn back to chapter three and see how you can check this result by your own or other people's observation of you. When you have done this, record your self/other validation result below.

Result of validation by self/other observation:

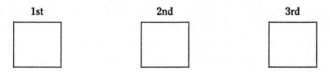

1st   2nd   3rd

(The interest test is used by permission of Hatters Lane Publications, copyright Gordon Jones 1990.)

Actions Card Sort
See pages 159-70.

Research (find out)	**Operate** (machines/equipment)
Lead (people)	**Select** (make choices)
Attach (materials/parts)	**Facilitate** (enable)
Analyze (classify/discriminate)	**Make good use of**
Encourage	**Evaluate** (judge/measure)

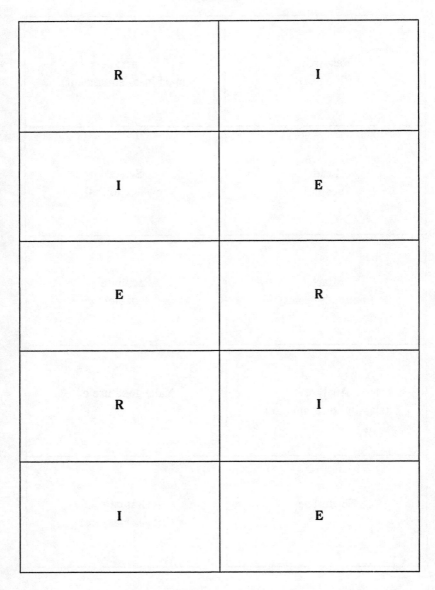

Install (equipment/machines)	**Arrange** (events/activities/meetings)
Gather information	**Use tools** (household equipment/ spanner/saw)
Develop (ideas/people/procedures)	**Test** (data/methods)
Replace (worn parts, etc.)	**Influence** (people/organizations)
Design (methods/systems)	**Move/transport**

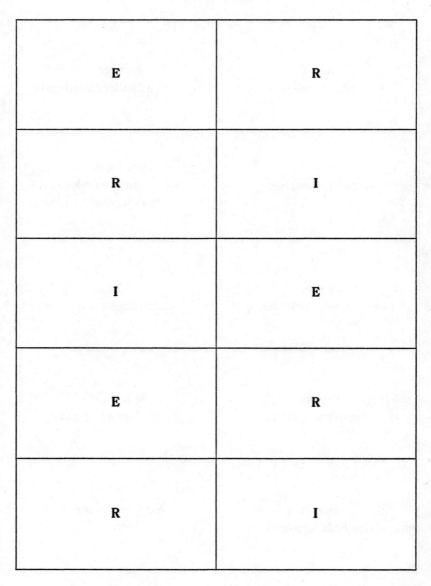

E	R
R	I
I	E
E	R
R	I

Motivate (stimulate)	**Examine** (investigatively)
Construct (with materials)	**Plan** (prepare/foresee)
Observe (examine/take note)	**Repair**
Coordinate (between people and groups)	**Photograph**
Care for	**Record** (data/figures)

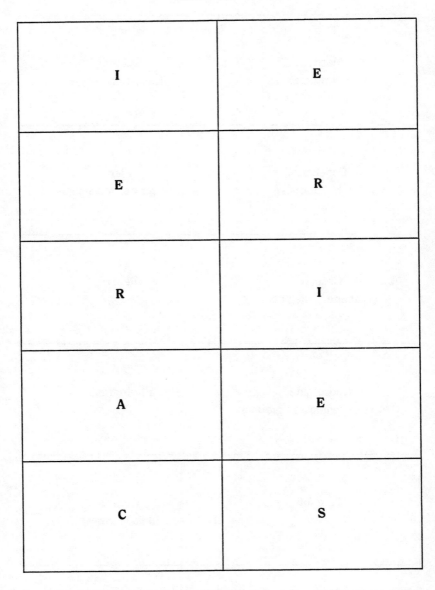

I	E
E	R
R	I
A	E
C	S

Design (forms/clothes/buildings)	Teach/train
Summarize (sum up, review)	**Write**
Understand (people)	**Monitor** (check, keep track of)
Interpret (language/data)	**Recognize** (values/insight/need)
Organize (events/data—not people)	Communicate

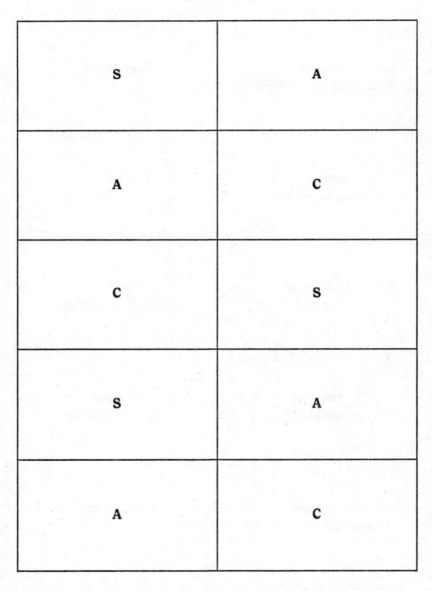

S	A
A	C
C	S
S	A
A	C

Recommend (people/action)	**Control** (systems/procedures—not people)
Express (self)	**Listen to**
Compare (performances/results/statistics)	**Express** (ideas)
Interact (with people)	**Prepare** (budget/agenda/schedule)
Create (originate, dream up)	**Relate to**

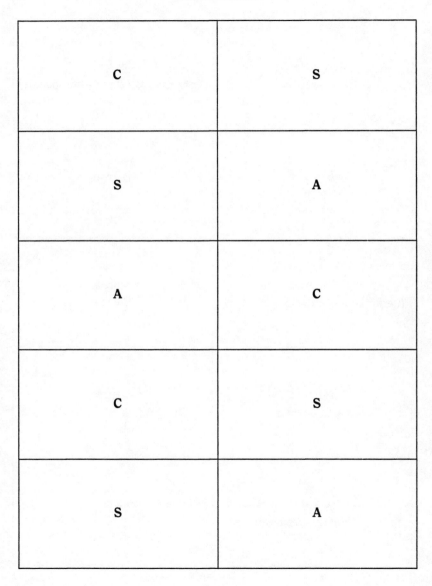

C	S
S	A
A	C
C	S
S	A

Calculate (numbers)	**Portray** (represent, picture)
Empathize (feel with)	**Clarify** (simplify, make clear)
1	2
3	4
5	6

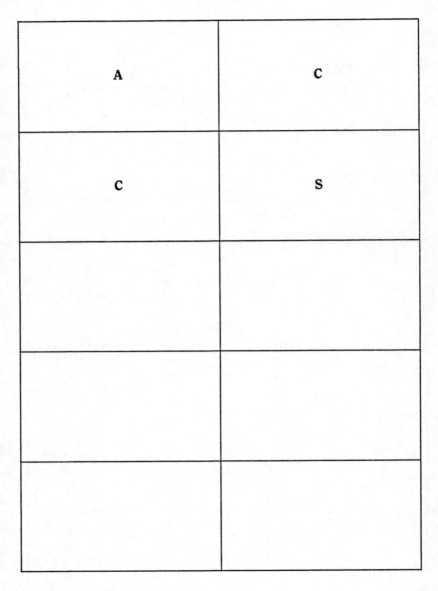

A	**C**
C	**S**

Appendix 4

Job Titles by Interest Themes

• • •

Job titles with adjacent interest themes:

RI Electrician
RI Forester
RI Office machine technician
RI Pilot (ship/airplane)

IR Radiographer
IR Civil engineer
IR Typesetting specialist
IR Systems analyst

IA Anthropologist
IA Technical journal editor
IA Architect
IA Linguist: translator

AI Art critic
AI Librarian
AI Lawyer
AI Publicity writer

AS Playwright/lyricist
AS Video editor
AS Artist (illustration)
AS Drama teacher

SA Foreign language teacher
SA Social worker
SA Kindergarten teacher
SA Minister

SE Receptionist

SE School administrator

SE Counselor

SE Housing officer

ES Personnel manager

ES Public relations officer

ES Sales representative

ES Business manager

EC Purchasing agent

EC Shipping manager

EC Retail store manager

EC Insurance agent

CE Production planner

CE Office manager

CE Customs inspector

CE Cost accountant

CR Traffic warden

CR Machine operator

CR Agricultural worker

CR Assembly line worker

RC Carpenter

RC Truck driver

RC Window cleaner

RC Toolmaker

Those with alternate themes:

RA Decorator

RA Occupational therapist

RA Engraver

AR Sculptor

AR Sign writer

AR Cake decorator

IS Physics teacher

IS Medical doctor

IS Psychologist

SI Nurse

SI Adult literacy specialist

SI Careers officer

AE Advertising executive

AE Journalist

AE TV/film script writer

EA Antique dealer

EA Film producer

EA Music director

SC School welfare assistant

SC Nursing assistant

SC Dental assistant

CS Cashier

CS Librarian

CS Telephone operator

ER Printshop manager   RE Maintenance supervisor
ER Building work estimator   RE Construction foreman
ER Military (NCO)   RE Canteen manager

CI Treasurer   IC Research assistant
CI Bibliographer   IC Computer operator
CI Proofreader   IC Management analyst

Those with opposite themes:

RS Police officer   SR PE teacher
RS Hardware storekeeper   SR Rural development officer

IE Pharmacist   EI Computer software sales
                                  manager
IE Meteorologist   EI Foreign exchange dealer

AC Cartographer   CA Window dresser

Note: Many people who have different interest codes to the above jobs can do them successfully. The fact that you have a particular interest code does not mean that you will automatically do the indicated job well. There are many other factors involved, as the other chapters in this book indicate. The above examples are only to help give an idea of how the interest themes combine in certain types of job.

Appendix 5

Natural
Aptitudes
Addendum

• • •

Identifying Natural Aptitudes by Classification
In order to identify natural aptitudes without resorting to very sophisticated tests, there is a second measure that can be used. This is a card sort method. It considers the degree of satisfaction you get from using certain skills and then looks at your level of proficiency in these.

It is necessary to use both means of classification (satisfaction and proficiency) because it is possible to enjoy doing something without being particularly good at it. A natural aptitude may lie dormant due to lack of opportunities to use it, or because it can only be used with other skills or training. For example, you may be a natural gardener but not be able to do gardening because you have no garden, and cannot go into agriculture because you have no training in that discipline.

The following is a list of natural aptitudes with which we are going to work.

Be "up front"—perform, speak publicly, be MC, demonstrate.

Empathize—understand, listen, draw out, accept.

Advise—guide, recommend, give counsel, suggest.

Teach—instruct, inform, facilitate learning, tutor.

Write—reports, letters, articles.

Express creatively—write, act, draw, paint, sculpt, play music, dance, compose music.

Conceive—invent, design, have ideas, visualize, conceptualize, picture.

Develop—from ideas and concepts to functional systems, develop objects, adapt, implement, modify.

Organize—schedule, plan, arrange, coordinate, set goals.

Research—investigate, find out, inquire, gather data, survey, interview.

Examine—measure, check, try out, evaluate, assess.

Analyze—break down, categorize, group systematically, resolve logically, evaluate.

Mediate—reconcile, make peace, intercede, arbitrate.

Bargain—negotiate, come to agreement, reach compromise.

Liaise—stimulate communication, act as link, relate to.

Monitor—observe, review, keep track of.

Supervise—oversee, direct, govern, command, lead, manage, administer.

Motivate—inspire, stimulate, mobilize, promote, influence.

Troubleshoot—expedite, solve, make it work.

Persuade—convince, sell, influence, promote.

Host/hostess—entertain, look after, make welcome, be hospitable.

Run the system—record, keep data, enter-up, tabulate, collate, follow procedures.

Economize—budget, use resources well, save resources.

Check—proofread, edit, assess quality, make sure it's right.

Tend—care for, nurse, nurture, heal (animals or people).

Use manual dexterity—as in household duties, operate equipment, build, construct.

Use muscular coordination—walk, throw, balance, catch, hit, run.

Engage in practical activity—bake, decorate, sew.

Engage in agricultural operations—grow plants and food, prune, weed, fertilize.

Show foresight—predict, plan ahead.

It is not an exhaustive list, so you may want to add other skills that you feel are appropriate to you. The thirty natural aptitudes together with eight head cards (five measuring satisfaction level, three measuring skill level) are laid out below. You have two options for producing a set of natural aptitude cards.

1. Photocopy them from the book and cut them up.

2. Copy them by hand onto notecards or paper and cut them up.

Now you have a set of cards or slips of paper to do the natural aptitude card sort. First, sort the cards according to the degree of skill you feel you have by placing the aptitude cards under one of the three headcards: Accomplished, Able or Unskilled.

Second, divide each of the three piles of cards according to how much you enjoy using each aptitude, using the following five levels of satisfaction—delight in using, always get pleasure in using, usually enjoy using, like to use occasionally and not happy using. The head cards are also graded with numbers. Some of you may find it easier to use the numbers to determine your degree of skill or satisfaction than to use the descriptions.

You should now have fifteen piles of cards, providing you have aptitudes you wish to categorize under the fifteen sections. Copy this information onto paper so that you have a chart like the table below, which shows how the page should be set out. You may not wish to use the major heading from the cards if this does not most accurately describe your aptitude (or lack of aptitude) in that area. You can use the heading plus one of the other descriptions or use one or two of the other descriptions. So, for example, when recording the *"Empathize*—understand, listen, draw-out, accept" card, you may feel that "empathize/listen" describes your aptitude best. Someone else might use "understand/accept."

	Accomplished 3	Able 2	Unskilled 1
Delight in using 5			
Always get pleasure in using 4			
Usually enjoy using 3			
Like to use occasionally 2			
Not happy using 1			

Analyzing a Natural Aptitudes Chart

You now need to examine your natural aptitudes chart to find out just what your natural aptitudes are and whether you have some that you have not developed. Perhaps with some further training you could develop these to give you a more satisfying lifestyle. First let us consider the hypothetical chart of someone we will call Fred.

Fred's Natural Aptitudes Chart

	Accomplished 3	Able 2	Unskilled 1
Delight in using 5	analyze/resolve logically research/investigate	empathize/listen instruct/tutor	tend/care for engage in practical activity host/look after
Always get pleasure in using 4	conceive/visualize develop	use manual dexterity monitor/observe	express creatively grow plants liaise
Usually enjoy using 3		examine/assess use muscular coordination advise/guide	write reports economize/save resources
Like to use occasionally 2		predict/plan ahead check/proofread record/keep data	organize/arrange be up front mediate/reconcile
Not happy to use 1		motivate/inspire persaude/convince supervise/direct	troubleshoot bargain/negotiate

Fred is a highly competent computer programmer and systems analyst. He is fairly introverted and has lived for his work, putting in long hours at his computer. He feels that his computing is taking over his life and, although he is using his natural aptitudes (analyzing, researching, visualizing, developing), he is ill at ease about himself and his work.

His company wants him to take more responsibility for the computer department, but the managerial skills of supervising, motivating, organizing and planning ahead are ones that he is not happy using or prefers to use only occasionally. At work, an alternative for Fred would be to become an instructor of others.

He is technically very good, and enjoys teaching and training. He could improve his teaching skills and either help his own or other departments by training people in computer programming and systems analysis. This would be more satisfying for him than moving up the managerial ladder.

Fred has several indicators on the chart (empathize/listen, instruct/ tutor, tend/care for) that show that he likes helping people and will probably get deeper satisfaction from doing this than from directing and managing a department.

Fred could think about developing other areas of his life. It has revolved almost exclusively around his major skills until now. The "engage in practical activity" and "use manual dexterity" suggest that he has some Realistic (R) interests. He could take an evening class in car maintenance to enable him to service his own car, or a class in a craft like wood-carving, which he may find very relaxing. The latter would combine his practical skills with his "express creatively," which also gives him pleasure. This will mean that computing will become only a part of his life, instead of being the whole of it, and his enthusiasm for it may be revived.

"Host/look after" is another aptitude that he might like to use more by taking further training and/or reading about the subject. This combined with his practical abilities may lead him to take up cooking and entertaining. His wife may be only too willing for him to share the cooking (and the cleaning) so that he can gain experience, and when he has grown in confidence at home he may feel able to offer his help to the church catering team. Maybe he can join the church welcome team.

Analyzing Your Natural Aptitudes Chart

Look at your own chart and pay particular attention to the natural aptitudes that you enjoy but have not developed. You could, like Fred, take training in these and begin to use them at home or in the church. For example, you may have "play music" in this category. Perhaps your education never gave you the opportunity to learn beyond a certain level, or maybe you live in an apartment where you can't practice. It's never too late to begin. You will get a lot of fun out of this and it may be used in your church once you've achieved a certain level of proficiency. You may never be a Yehudi Menuhin and you may never earn your living with it, but you can enhance your worship and your relaxation.

If you're in a job where you feel frustrated and you think you are underachieving, there may be some items in the "Delight in using" row and "Accomplished" column that could be used to greater advantage. For instance, if you are a skilled carpenter and builder with a high degree of competence in design but you are concentrating solely on the practical side, you might feel more fulfilled if you expanded your field of work to include more design.

It is possible that in completing your chart you have underestimated your aptitudes and don't have anything under the heading "Accomplished." This doesn't matter. It is the pattern of the chart that is important, and if you have as your highest level of competence "Able," then, for the purpose of analysis, treat it as if it were "Accomplished."

Perhaps as you have worked through this exercise you have begun to know yourself a little better—what your natural aptitudes really are. Compare the results of this second exercise with that in chapter five. Are you beginning to see where your natural aptitudes lie? Are there some that you would like to develop further? Often it is not so much the job we do as the skills we use in doing it that brings satisfaction.

Review
Examining your natural aptitudes by card sort classification will have given you more data. Add this to your folder now, together with any thoughts you may have had concerning possible actions you could take.

Natural Aptitudes Card Sort

Be "up front"— perform, speak publicly, be MC, demonstrate	Tend—care for nurse, nurture, heal (animals or people)
Empathize— understand, listen, draw out, accept	Use manual dexterity— as in household duties, operate equipment, build, construct
Write—reports, articles, letters	Use muscular coordination— walk, throw, balance, catch, hit, run

Express creatively—write, act, draw, paint, sculpt, play music, dance, compose music	**Engage in practical activity**—bake, decorate, sew
Conceive—invent, design, have ideas, visualize, conceptualize, picture	**Engage in agricultural activity**—grow plants and food, prune, weed, fertilize
Develop—from ideas and concepts to functional systems, develop objects, adapt, implement, modify	**Teach**—instruct, inform, facilitate learning, tutor
Organize—schedule, plan, arrange, coordinate, set goals	**Advise**—guide, recommend, give counsel, suggest

Research— investigate, find out, inquire, gather data, survey, interview	**Show foresight—** predict, plan ahead
Analyze—break down, categorize, group systematically, resolve logically, evaluate	**Monitor—**observe, review, keep track of
Mediate—reconcile, make peace, intercede, arbitrate	**Examine—**measure, check, try out, evaluate, assess
Bargain—negotiate, come to agreement, reach compromise	**Check—**proofread, edit, assess quality, make sure it's right

Liaise—stimulate communication, act as link, relate to	**Economize**—budget, use resources well, save resources
Supervise—oversee, direct, lead, govern, command, manage, administer	**Accomplished**—expert, very proficient 3
Motivate—inspire, stimulate, mobilize, promote, influence	**Able**—competent, capable, adept 2
Troubleshoot—expedite, solve, make it work	**Unskilled**—inability in, not competent 1

Persuade—convince, sell, influence, promote	Delight in using 5
Host/hostess—entertain, look after, make welcome, be hospitable	Always get pleasure in using 4
Run the system—record, keep data, enter-up, tabulate, collate, follow procedures	Usually enjoy using 3
Like to use occasionally 2	Not happy using 1

Appendix 6

Values Card Sort

• • •

Promotion—opportunities to move ahead swiftly, gaining advancement and seniority	**Originality**—opportunity for free expression and creativity
Adventure—risk-taking often involved in the work role	**Competition**—opportunity to contend against others, striving to be the best
Challenge—demanding tasks or complex questions, problem solving or troubleshooting	**Variety**—work content and setting that change often

Pressure—circumstances that demand high-pace activity and work done rapidly	**Service**—helping other people directly, either practically or spiritually
Proficiency—exercising competence, showing high level of effectiveness	**Friendships**—opportunities to develop close personal relationships at work
Autonomy—being free to be independent and able to determine own activities	**Material gain**— the likelihood of high earnings
Influence—being in a position to affect or change other people's opinions	**Help society**—showing social responsibility, helping the community

Academic status—being acknowledged as intellectually able and scholarly	**Compatible colleagues**—working with those who share similar beliefs and values
Leadership—having the power to decide policies, courses of action, and to be responsible for people	**Self-growth**—opportunities to make the most of self, to develop full potential
Stability—work that is predictable and not likely to change	**Prestige**—gaining the respect of others because of job status
Work alone—working mostly without contact with others	**Research**—work to expand frontiers of knowledge

Family—work that does not encroach on or upset family life	**Peaceful atmosphere**—lack of pressure
Security—work in which job tenure and long-term prospects and pension are good	**Spiritual and moral fulfillment**—contributing toward the achievement of spiritual and moral ideals
Physical challenge—needing to use bodily strength, speed or agility	**Balance**—a well-adjusted lifestyle between work and the rest of life
Order—preferring to do one thing at a time	**Association**—lots of opportunity for contact with people

Work with others— working with a close team of colleagues	**Location**—in the geographical place where you wish to live
Artistic expression— expressing by writing, drama, painting, music, etc.	**Aesthetics**—working in a pleasing environment and/or studying beautiful things
add your own values	add your own values
add your own values	add your own values

Appendix 7

Learning
Type
Test

• • •

Thinking of yourself in a learning environment, award yourself points as follows: 2 = mostly true, 1 = not sure, 0 = mostly untrue.

Try not to use the "not sure" category unless it is absolutely necessary and you really cannot make up your mind. Everyone can identify with each of these statements in some measure. We are looking at your preferences. It is best to go by your "gut" reaction and not spend too long pondering over the statements.

_____ 1. I naturally empathize with others.

_____ 2. I enjoy social events and activities.

_____ 3. Being is more important to me than doing.

_____ 4. I like excitement in life.

_____ 5. I test out ideas to see if they are true.

_____ 6. I am interested in science, math and research.

_____ 7. I prefer dealing with things rather than with people.

_____ 8. I prefer to learn cooperatively with others.

_____ 9. I like to see things managed well.

_____ 10. I am sensitive to other people's needs.

_____ 11. I prepare thoroughly.

_____ 12. I like to "get down to business" quickly.

_____ 13. I am more affected by feelings than by logic.

_____ 14. I am a pragmatist and a realist.

_____ 15. I can be demanding of myself and others.

_____ 16. I share my feelings easily.

_____ 17. Principles are more important to me than practices.

_____ 18. I like to make things happen.

_____ 19. I see myself as impartial and objective.

_____ 20. I often reach right conclusions without using logical thinking.

_____ 21. I am more affected by logic than by feelings.

_____ 22. I particularly value harmonious relationships.

_____ 23. I enjoy solving problems.

_____ 24. I am attracted to novel ideas.

_____ 25. I often act spontaneously.

_____ 26. I like things to be useful (utilitarian).

_____ 27. I like to ponder and meditate on problems.

_____ 28. I like to investigate and puzzle through problems.

_____ 29. I quickly notice impractical and unfeasible suggestions.

_____ 30. I strive for academic excellence.

_____ 31. I am attracted to the humanities and social sciences.

_____ 32. I like to try things out actively.

_____ 33. Freedom of action is important to me.

_____ 34. I am analytical.

_____ 35. I am interested in theoretical concepts.

_____ 36. I look for new ways of doing things.

_____ 37. I can see the practical solution.

_____ 38. I am cautious and reflective.

_____ 39. I enjoy observing others' behavior.

_____ 40. I like the teacher/instructor to be firmly in control.

_____ 41. I think rules and regulations are important.

_____ 42. I am irritated by careless thinking.

_____ 43. I like to be where the action is.

_____ 44. I thrive on challenges.

_____ 45. I like discussions to be rational.

_____ 46. I am practical and noted for my common sense.

_____ 47. I like to apply ideas and see them working.

_____ 48. I am a risk taker.

_____ 49. I am painstaking and thorough in my work.

_____ 50. I am friendly and gregarious.

_____ 51. I am attracted to selling and the entertainment business.

_____ 52. The underlying meaning is important to me.

_____ 53. I like to link new data to established theory.

_____ 54. I reach decisions after careful thought.

_____ 55. I value the opinions of experts.

_____ 56. I control my emotions.

_____ 57. Working hard is important to me.

_____ 58. I like to keep to the agenda.

_____ 59. I like collecting information.

_____ 60. I take others' views into account.

_____ 61. I seek to influence others.

_____ 62. I dislike competition in a learning environment.

_____ 63. I get enthusiastic about projects.

_____ 64. I am grounded in reality and am down-to-earth.

_____ 65. I like to serve and be useful.

_____ 66. I hold my opinions firmly.

_____ 67. I like to experiment and see if things work.

_____ 68. I tend to "think through" rather than "act spontaneously."

_____ 69. I learn by trial and error.

_____ 70. I bring structure and order to my work.

_____ 71. I like to look at all aspects.

_____ 72. I seek variety in what I do.

_____ 73. I am innovative in my approach to problems.

_____ 74. I tend to listen more than speak.

_____ 75. I value sequential thinking.

_____ 76. I like to be productive.

_____ 77. I like to use my imagination.

_____ 78. I like applied sciences, business and engineering.

_____ 79. I am disciplined in my personal life.

_____ 80. Being authentic is important to me.

Your Learning Type Test Results—Scoring the Inventory

Indicate, beside each question below, the number of points you awarded to each question of the inventory. Add the figures in each column to obtain the four totals.

Learning Type Orientation

Meaning	Theory	Solution	Activity
1. _____	5. _____	7. _____	2. _____
3. _____	6. _____	9. _____	4. _____
8. _____	15. _____	11. _____	16. _____
10. _____	17. _____	12. _____	18. _____
13. _____	19. _____	14. _____	20. _____
22. _____	21. _____	23. _____	24. _____
27. _____	28. _____	26. _____	25. _____
31. _____	30. _____	29. _____	32. _____
38. _____	34. _____	37. _____	33. _____
39. _____	35. _____	40. _____	36. _____
49. _____	42. _____	41. _____	43. _____
52. _____	45. _____	46. _____	44. _____
54. _____	53. _____	47. _____	48. _____
59. _____	55. _____	56. _____	50. _____
60. _____	58. _____	57. _____	51. _____
62. _____	66. _____	64. _____	61. _____
71. _____	68. _____	65. _____	63. _____
74. _____	70. _____	67. _____	69. _____
77. _____	75. _____	76. _____	72. _____
80. _____	79. _____	78. _____	73. _____

Totals _____   _____   _____   _____

Your Learning Type Test Results

	Meaning	Theory	Solution	Activity

Learning type
orientation:
(column totals)

Self-observation
result:
(from chapter
seven)

Considering these results, from the test and by self-observation, which do you think is really you, or are you somewhere "in between"? It's up to you to decide and thereby validate your result.

	Meaning	Theory	Solution	Activity
Your validated result:				

Plotting Your Result

Plot the validated result on the diagonal axes as shown in the example, and shade in the area of each square. The area of each square is the percentage of that learning type that you prefer to use. The degree to which you use each of the four learning types is your style of learning.

EXAMPLE

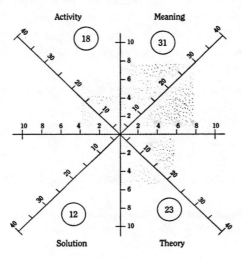

YOUR RESULT

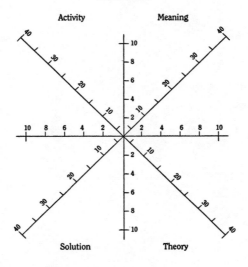

Working the learning type percentages from the example, simply square by multiplying the readings on the horizontal and vertical axes: Meaning $8 \times 8 = 64\%$, Theory $6 \times 6 = 36\%$, Solution $3 \times 3 = 9\%$, Activity $5 \times 5 = 25\%$. Now work your own and record below.

Note: These percentages are percentages of each quadrant and do not add up to 100%.

My learning style:

Meaning _____ % Theory _____ % Solution _____ % Activity _____ %

Published by Hatters Lane Publications, High Wycombe, Bucks. HP13 7LY, England. Copyright Gordon and Rosemary Jones, 1990 (revised edition 1992).

Appendix 8

Self/Other Esteem
Measure

• • •

This little test will help you get a better idea of how you see yourself and how you see others. Answer each question as honestly as you can. Rate yourself on each question using this numbering system:

Definitely or almost always—3
Probably or often—2
Probably not or seldom—1
Definitely not or almost never—0

Self-esteem Measure

_____ 1. I am truly content with the way I look.
_____ 2. I feel positive about facing new challenges.
_____ 3. I consider my ability to think and reason adequate.
_____ 4. I think people enjoy being with me.
_____ 5. I am satisfied with the degree of success I'm experiencing so far in my life.

_____ 6. I feel as worthwhile when I'm just having a good time as when I'm doing something constructive.

_____ 7. I consistently forgive myself when I make mistakes.

_____ 8. When I make a mistake I refrain from telling myself negative things (such as "I'm stupid, clumsy, can't do anything right, etc.").

_____ 9. I can honestly say that I love myself.

_____ 10. Deep down I feel that God accepts me just the way I am.

_____ 11. When I look at myself in the mirror I'm happy with what I see.

_____ 12. I feel competent to tackle most new jobs.

_____ 13. I am genuinely happy with my intellectual ability.

_____ 14. I feel good about my personality.

_____ 15. Overall I regard myself as successful in life.

_____ 16. I feel of great value and worth to God, even when I fail.

_____ 17. When I do something wrong or unwise I quickly get over being angry with myself.

_____ 18. My thoughts toward myself are usually positive rather than critical.

_____ 19. I appreciate myself even though I'm not perfect.

_____ 20. Though I realize I'm a sinner, deep down I can truly feel that God sees me as holy and blameless through Christ.

_____ Self-esteem total score

Compare your self-esteem score with the comments below.

Total Score	Comments
56-60	If you scored in this range you may have faked the test or you may see yourself more highly than you ought. It's also possible that you have an excellent self-esteem.
46-55	You seem to have a high estimation of yourself and should

	have few problems in self-esteem.
36-45	Overall you appear to be neither high nor low in self-esteem but there may be specific areas which need attention.
26-35	There is room for improvement in the degree to which you esteem yourself.
0-25	If you were honest in the test you have a real need for improvement in your esteem of yourself.

Note: If you scored low do not assume that you have a low opinion of yourself. No test of this nature can adequately describe the self-esteem of every person who takes it. If you scored below 25 you may want to talk it over with a friend or a Christian counselor. You may be helped by looking at the particular questions on which you scored low and which can indicate particular aspects of how you view yourself and in which you may need help.

Other-esteem Measure

_____ 1. I feel other people are trustworthy.

_____ 2. Other people are significant to me.

_____ 3. I feel other people are competent.

_____ 4. I feel included in other people's activities.

_____ 5. The amount others influence me is satisfactory to me.

_____ 6. I feel appreciated by others.

_____ 7. I am happy with the degree to which other people are open with me.

_____ 8. People know the real me.

_____ 9. I am happy with the degree of authority I assert over others.

_____ 10. I am rarely irritated with other people.

_____ 11. People can be depended on.

_____ 12. Other people are a meaningful part of my life.

_____ 13. I can rely on other people's capabilities.

_____ 14. I am accepted by the group.

_____ 15. I am happy with the degree to which others control me.

_____ 16. Most people like me.

_____ 17. Others share their feelings with me as much as I desire.

_____ 18. People understand me.

_____ 19. My control of others is acceptable to them.

_____ 20. In general other people do not annoy me.

_____ Other-esteem total score

Compare your other-esteem result with the comments below.

Total score	Comments
56-60	If you scored in this range you may have an idealistic view of other people. It's also possible that you have faked the test or do esteem others very highly.
46-55	You seem to have a high esteem for others, and should have few problems accepting them.
36-45	Overall you appear to be neither high nor low in your esteem for others.
26-35	There is room for improvement in the degree to which you esteem others.
0-25	If you were honest in the test you have a real need for improvement in your esteem for others.

Note: If you scored low do not assume that you have an inadequate relationship with others. No test of this nature can adequately describe the degree to which we esteem others. If you scored below 25 you may want to talk it over with a friend or a Christian counselor. You may be helped by looking at the particular questions on which you scored low and which can indicate particular aspects of your relationship with others in which you may need help.

Appendix 9

Sample Profile

• • •

In order to help you to write your own personal profile from the data you have kept in your personal results folder, here is a sample profile.

My Personal Profile
Mary Smith
Date

1. Interests
From the interest test and by self-evaluation my interests are best described as:

Enterprising (E)

Artistic (A)

Social (S)

The Enterprising theme is my strongest and I demonstrate this theme when I lead people or liaise or negotiate with them. I also have some of the "Entrepreneur" in my makeup.

The Artistic theme scores second and it expresses itself in my interest in drama and creative writing, and in expressing myself in an individual way.

The Social theme shows itself in my desire to be involved in group discussion and in using my Enterprising and Artistic gifts to help other people.

I do not appear to have much interest in the Investigative (I) theme. As this is my weakest area, I should be careful about taking on activities that involve its use. In particular, work requiring a lot of painstaking analysis or mathematical or scientific abilities may cause me difficulty.

2. Natural Aptitudes

A. By examining the pattern of accomplishments that gave me deep satisfaction I have identified the following natural aptitudes:

1. My natural way of managing my life is to—
   choose/decide   think through/plan
2. My natural way of interacting with people is to—
   get together/discuss/share   persuade/negotiate   motivate/inspire
3. I handle the world about me (data, ideas, things) by—
   writing/speaking   drawing/expressing creatively
   scheduling/planning
4. The sort of environments in which I operate most happily are—
   innovative   goal oriented   school/church/communal
5. The sort of objects I normally work on or with are—
   ideas/people/books/words/poetry   plans/programs
6. My primary role and style when engaged in natural achievements is—
   Role: entrepreneur (What I do)
   Style: creator (How I go about it)
7. What motivates me to achieve is—
   expressing myself creatively (Why I do it)

B. By using the natural aptitudes card sort and building a natural aptitudes chart I have identified the following:
1. Natural aptitudes that I enjoy using and in which I am accomplished
are—
   proofread/edit   motivate   sell   write
2. Natural aptitudes that I enjoy using but could increase my ability by
further training/use are—
   negotiate   expedite   perceive   intuitively initiate change
3. Natural aptitudes that I do not really possess and therefore do not enjoy
using and that I should be careful not to build into my permanent lifestyle
more than is necessary are—
   maintain records   estimate   analyze   test

3. Values
By using the values card sort, the following values appear to be the most
important to me in my work—
   creative expression   affiliation   fast pace   work with others
   challenging problems   change and variety   influence people
   make decisions
The values that are least important to me in my work are—
   precision work   work alone   physical challenge   status   stability
   high earnings
The values that have motivated me in my most memorable achievements
are—
   achieving together   overcoming the difficulties
I have checked my present job and general lifestyle against both my most
important and my least important values.

4. Personality Type
People see me as warm and high spirited and as I am fairly extraverted
I spend a lot of time with people. At work I see myself as having flair and

imagination. I work in bursts of creative energy but can lose interest in the follow-through stage. People around me generally know how I feel as I am very expressive. I can't hide my feelings even if I want to.

5. Learning Style

My natural learning style can be described as thinking/doing. I gather information and data by thinking. I seek to use it by trying it out and applying it to the world about me. I can apply my knowledge of my preferred learning style as follows:

☐ In my Sunday-school class, remembering that the children may not be analytical learners. I must try to get them involved in using the things we learn and in doing things themselves.

☐ In my training, where I may need to hold back my desire to apply what I have learned in order to reflect on the theory a little more and see the whole picture before putting it to practical use.

6. Life Changes

Where I am in my life's journey.

1. Personal life—I have a wide circle of friends but feel the need to develop a few to much greater depth. In particular I feel I need a close friend to pray with and share with more deeply.

2. Spiritual life—My extravert personality means I spend lots of time with people and on active pursuits. I want to start developing my inner life with the Lord, spending less time on Christian activities and more time with him.

3. Family life (Mary is single.)—I need to discuss with Mom and Dad and my brother and sister what I have discovered about my values, gifts and personality type. I can now see why some family misunderstandings have occurred. I want my family relationships to come into line with my new understanding of them and of myself.

4. Church life—See note above about Sunday school.

5. Work—I need to go and see my boss and discuss my present job to see if there is any possibility of using my creative gifts a little more.

6. Roles—The roles that God has called me to at this point in my life are—

child of God   a member of St. Cuthbert's   colleague   friend
daughter   sister

Gordon and Rosemary Jones would be pleased to hear from anyone who completes the exercises and writes up their profile. Send them a copy of your completed profile, c/o the publisher, and they will reply, although they cannot guarantee to comment on each profile.

Notes

Chapter 2
[1]Ralph T. Mattson and Arthur F. Miller, *Finding a Job You Can Love* (New York: Thomas Nelson, 1982).
[2]Marketing and Research Corporation, New Jersey, 1976.
[3]Mattson and Miller, *Finding a Job.*

Chapter 3
[1]Gary D. Gottfredson, John L. Holland and Deborah Kimiko Ogawa, *Dictionary of Holland Occupational Codes* (Palo Alto, Calif.: Consulting Psychologists Press, 1982).

Chapter 5
[1]Louis Raths, Merrill Harmin and Sidney B. Simon, *Values and Teaching* (Columbus, Ohio: Charles E. Merrill, 1966).

Chapter 6
[1]Isabel B. Myers and Katharine Briggs, *Myers Briggs Type Indicator.*
[2]Harold Grant et al., *From Image to Likeness* (New York: Paulist Press, 1983).
[3]David Keirsey and Marilyn Bates, *Please Understand Me* (Del Mar, Calif.: Prometheus Nemesis, 1984).
[4]Ibid.

Chapter 7
[1]David Kolb, *Experiential Learning—Experience as the Source of Learning and Development* (Englewood Cliffs, N.J.: Prentice Hall, 1984).

[2]Bernice McCarthy, *The 4 MAT System* (Barrington, Ill.: Excel, 1980).

Chapter 8
[1]Allen Tough, *Self-planned Learning and Major Personal Change,* in "Adult Learning: Issues and Innovations," ERIC Clearing House in Career Education, N. Illinois University, 1976.

Chapter 9
[1]Thomas Harris, *I'm OK—You're OK* (Old Tappan, N.J.: Fleming H. Revell, 1976).
[2]John M. Cleese, "Careers—No More Mistakes and You're Through!" *Forbes,* 16 May 1988.

Chapter 10
[1]John Buckeridge, "Christians at Work—How to Juggle Work, Rest and Play," *21st Century Christian,* February 1990.